BIRDS

S of an Francisco
and the Bay Area

Chris C. Fisher
Joseph Morlan

LONE PINE

D0052568

The Publisher: Lone Pine Publishing

16149 Redmond Way, #180	202A, 1110 Seymour Street	206, 10426 – 81 Avenue
Redmond, Washington	Vancouver, British Columbia	Edmonton, Alberta
U.S.A. 98052	Canada V6B 3N3	Canada T6E 1X5

Canadian Cataloguing in Publication Data

Fisher, Chris C. (Christopher Charles)
    Birds of San Francisco and the Bay area

    Includes bibliographical references and index.
    ISBN 1-55105-080-3

    1. Birds—California—San Francisco—Identification. 2. Bird watching—California—San Francisco. 3. Birds—California—San Francisco Bay Area—Identification. 4. Bird watching— California—San Francisco Bay Area. I. Morlan, Joseph. II. Title.
QL684.C2F57 1996   598.29794'6   C96-910608-4

Senior Editor: Nancy Foulds
Editorial: Roland Lines, Jennifer Keane
Design and Layout: Carol S. Dragich
Cover Design: Carol S. Dragich
Cover Illustration: Gary Ross
Technical Review: Wayne Campbell, Dennis Paulson
Separations and Film: Elite Lithographers Co. Ltd., Edmonton, Alberta, Canada
Printing: Quality Color Press Inc., Edmonton, Alberta, Canada

The checklist of San Mateo County birds (pp. 151–55) originally appeared in *San Francisco Peninsula Birdwatching* (Sequoia Audubon Society 1996). © 1996 by the Sequoia Audubon Society. Reprinted by permission of the publisher.

Illustration Credits

All illustrations are by **Gary Ross**, except as follows:
Ted Nordhagen: 1, 9 (top), 12 (2nd from top), 13 (middle & bottom), 17, 20, 24, 56, 65, 67, 83, 90, 96, 98, 105, 114, 140, 142 (top)
Ewa Pluciennik: 12 (top), 15 (middle), 18, 26, 38, 51, 69, 77, 81, 100, 104, 116, 125, 128, 135, 149 (bottom)
Horst Krause: 79, 146.

The publisher gratefully acknowledges the support of Alberta Community Development and the Department of Canadian Heritage.

Contents

Acknowledgments

A book such as this is made possible by the inspired work of San Francisco's naturalist community. Its contributions continue to advance the science of ornithology and to motivate a new generation of nature lovers.

My thanks to Gary Ross, Ewa Pluciennik, Ted Nordhagen and Horst Krause, whose illustrations have elevated the quality of this book; Carole Patterson for her continual support; the Sequoia Audubon Society (which provided the checklist) and the other Audubon Societies of the San Francisco area, which all make daily contributions to natural history; the team at Lone Pine Publishing—Shane Kennedy, Nancy Foulds, Roland Lines, Carol Dragich and Jennifer Keane—for their input and steering; and John Acorn and Jim Butler for their stewardship and their remarkable passion. Finally, my thanks go to Joe Morlan, Wayne Campbell and Dennis Paulson, premier naturalists whose works have served as models of excellence, for their thorough and helpful review of the text.

Chris C. Fisher

Introduction

No matter where we live, birds are a natural part of our lives. We are so used to seeing them that we often take their presence for granted. When we take the time to notice their colors, songs and behaviors, we experience their dynamic appeal.

This book presents a brief introduction into the lives of birds. It is intended to serve as a bird identification guide, and also as a bird appreciation guide. Getting to know the names of birds is the first step toward getting to know birds. Once we've made contact with a species, we can better appreciate its character and mannerisms during future encounters. Over a lifetime of meetings, many birds become acquaintances, some seen daily, others not for years.

The selection of species within this book represents a balance between the familiar and the noteworthy. Many of the 125 species described in this guide are the most common species found in the San Francisco area. Some are less common, but they are noteworthy because they are important ecologically or because their particular status grants them a high profile. It would be impossible for a beginners' book such as this to comprehensively describe all the birds found in the San Francisco region. Furthermore, there is no one site where all the species within this book can be observed simultaneously, but most species can be viewed—at least seasonally—within a short drive (or sail) from San Francisco. The San Francisco area is blessed with two excellent bird-finding guides (Richmond 1985, Sequoia Audubon Society 1996) that will help birders looking for a specific species.

It is hoped that this guide will inspire novice birdwatchers into spending some time outdoors, gaining valuable experience with the local bird community. This book stresses the identity of birds, but it also attempts to bring them to life by discussing their various character traits. We often discuss a bird's character traits in human terms, because personifying a bird's character can help us to feel a bond with the birds. The perceived links with birds should not be mistaken for actual behaviors, as our interpretations may falsely reflect the complexities of bird life.

FEATURES OF THE LANDSCAPE

The distribution of birdlife in the San Francisco area is greatly influenced by seasonality and habitat. The greatest diversity of birds occurs during the winter months as migrants from the north and from the interior retreat to San Francisco for the coast's moist and warm winter. Shorebirds line estuaries in San Francisco Bay and other shallow wetlands in impressive concentrations, feeding on the wealth of invertebrates living in the mudflats. Loons, grebes and waterfowl, frozen out of their summer breeding grounds, ride out the winter on the open ocean, on calm bays and on the lakes and ponds in the area.

Spring migration in the San Francisco area is a scattered affair. From mid-January until June, many different species of birds move through the region. Some of the first migrants are San Francisco's small Allen's Hummingbirds, returning in full force and joining the persistent Anna's Hummingbirds that remained. Through March and April, overwintering waterfowl and shorebirds gently trickle out of the Bay Area towards their far-off nesting grounds. By May, all but the last of the migrating songbirds have drifted through the area, using the corridor between the ocean and the cold coastal mountains as a freeway to the north. In May, the broadleaf forests seem alive with activity as sparrows and warblers move through the area; most of them continue on to the north.

Although most birds in the area are migratory, summers in the Bay Area still offer rewards for the persistent birder. Brown Pelicans return from the south and pose proudly on rocky outcrops along the coastline. Seabirds, cormorants and gulls, so common throughout most of the year, escape to secluded areas to nest. The Farallon Islands, offshore from San Francisco, is one such site, and hundreds of thousands of birds nest on these small rocky islands.

Nesting residents are tolerant of the hot and dry weather, and towhees and Bushtits raise their broods in parks and in the native oak, madrone and buckeye broadleaf forests. Wrentits, California Quail and Northern Mockingbirds cope well with the heat, raising their young in the coastal scrub and chaparral brushland. Swainson's Thrush joins the resident Winter Wrens and Brown Creepers in the humid coastal coniferous forests, where Douglas fir and coastal redwoods offer some protection from the hot bite of summer.

The fall migration begins shortly after the spring exodus closes. The first shorebirds begin to fly back through the Bay Area in early July, and their numbers peak through August. Many sandpipers and plovers remain, finding sufficient food in mud flats and estuaries to hold them until the spring. As birds move in a southerly direction in the fall, the southeasterly direction of the coastline of California creates migrant traps. Many birds build up in areas where they run into open ocean during their southerly flights. These areas offer some of the largest and most diverse concentrations of birds found around San Francisco. Hawk Hill at the Marin Headlands is one such example. Migrating raptors ride the updrafts of the headlands, gaining elevation before crossing the open waters of the Golden Gate. Although these same features funnel our smaller songbirds as well, their fall arrival may be best realized in backyards and city parks. In August, the trees and shrubs in these places once again come alive with the constant flitting of songbirds. These pockets of forest provide shelter for many species of birds, and as they are not busy with the task of reproduction through the winter, mixed species flocks often congregate in large numbers.

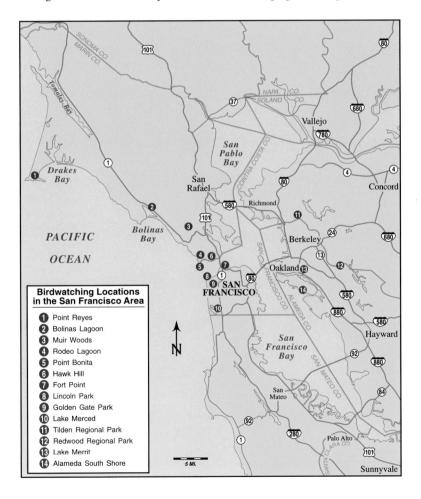

Birdwatching Locations in the San Francisco Area

1. Point Reyes
2. Bolinas Lagoon
3. Muir Woods
4. Rodeo Lagoon
5. Point Bonita
6. Hawk Hill
7. Fort Point
8. Lincoln Park
9. Golden Gate Park
10. Lake Merced
11. Tilden Regional Park
12. Redwood Regional Park
13. Lake Merrit
14. Alameda South Shore

THE IMPORTANCE OF HABITAT

Understanding the relationship between habitat and bird species often helps identify which birds are which. Because you won't find a loon up a tree or a quail out at sea, habitat is an important thing to note when bird-watching.

The quality of habitat is one of the most powerful factors to influence bird distribution, and with experience you may become amazed by the predictability of some birds within a specific habitat type. The habitat icons in this book show where each species can most commonly be found. It is important to realize, however, that because of their migratory habits, birds are sometimes found in completely different habitats.

Habitat Icons

Each bird in this guide is accompanied by at least one habitat symbol, which represents a general environment where the bird is most likely to be seen. Most birds will be seen within their associated habitat, but migrants can turn up in just about any habitat type. These unexpected surprises (despite being confusing to novice birders) are among the most powerful motivations for the increasing legion of birdwatchers.

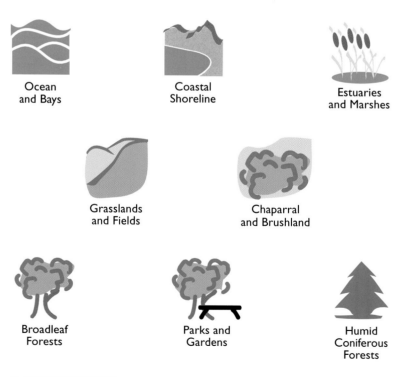

Ocean
and Bays

Coastal
Shoreline

Estuaries
and Marshes

Grasslands
and Fields

Chaparral
and Brushland

Broadleaf
Forests

Parks and
Gardens

Humid
Coniferous
Forests

THE ORGANIZATION OF THIS BOOK

To simplify field identification, *San Francisco Birds* is organized slightly differently from many other field guides that use strict phylogenetic groupings. In cases where many birds from the same family are described, conventional groupings are maintained. In other cases, however, distantly related birds that share physical and behavioral similarities are grouped together. This blend of family grouping and physically similar super-groups strives to help the novice birdwatcher identify and appreciate the birds he or she encounters.

DIVING BIRDS

loons, grebes, cormorants, etc.
These heavy-bodied birds are adapted to diving for their food. Between their under-water foraging dives, they are most frequently seen on the surface of the water. These birds could only be confused with one another or with certain diving ducks.

WETLAND WADERS

herons, egrets, coots
Although this group varies considerably in size, and represents two separate families of related birds, wetland waders share similar habitat and food preferences. Some of these long-legged birds of marshes are quite common, but certain species are heard far more than they are seen.

WATERFOWL

geese, ducks
Waterfowl tend to have stout bodies and webbed feet, and they are swift in flight. Although most species are associated with water, waterfowl can some-times be seen grazing on upland sites.

HAWKS AND FALCONS

osprey, hawks, falcons, etc.
From deep forests to open country to large lakes, there are hawks, kites and falcons hunting the skies. Their predatory look—with sharp talons, hooked bills and forward-facing eyes—easily identifies this group. Hawks generally forage during the day, and many use their broad wings to soar in thermals and updrafts.

QUAILS

These gamebirds bear a superficial resemblance to chickens. They are stout birds and poor flyers, and they are most often encountered on the ground or when flushed.

SHOREBIRDS

plovers, sandpipers, curlews, etc.
Shorebirds are usually confined to the shores and tidal flats of the ocean and bays. Although these small, long-legged, swift-flying birds are mainly found in our estuaries, don't be surprised to find certain species in pastures and marshy areas.

GULLS AND TERNS

Gulls are relatively large, usually light-colored birds that are frequently seen in the San Francisco area as they swim in salt- or freshwater, walk about in urban areas or soar gracefully over the city. Their backs tend to be darker than their bellies, and their feet are webbed. Terns are in the same family as gulls, but they are not often seen on the ground, they rarely soar and they have straight, pointed bills.

ALCIDS

murres, guillemots
These stocky, stubby-winged birds are found exclusively on the ocean or nesting on steep or isolated outcrops. They are relatively small, compact birds that swim underwater using their short, firm wings. They are poor fliers, and they need to beat their small wings quickly to stay airborne. 'Alcid' is a term used to denote a member of the auk family, to which these birds belong.

DOVES

All of San Francisco's doves are easily recognizable. Rock Doves are found in all urban areas, from city parks to the downtown core. These urban doves have many of the same physical and behavioral characteristics as the 'wilder' Band-tailed Pigeons and Mourning Doves.

OWLS

These night hunters have forward-facing eyes, a facial disk and a large, rounded head. Their feet are armed with powerful talons, and their bills are strongly hooked. Although owls are primarily active at night, their distinctive calls enable birdwatchers to readily identify them.

HUMMINGBIRDS

Hummingbirds are San Francisco's smallest birds, and their bright colors and swift flight are very characteristic.

KINGFISHERS

The kingfisher's behavior and physical characteristics are quite unlike any bird in San Francisco. It primarily hunts fish, plunging after them from the air or from an overhanging perch.

WOODPECKERS

The drumming sound of hammering wood and their precarious foraging habits easily identify most woodpeckers. They are frequently seen in forests, clinging to trunks and chipping away bark with their straight, sturdy bills. Even when these birds cannot be seen or heard, the characteristic marks of certain species can be seen on trees in any mature forest.

FLYCATCHERS

This family is perhaps best identified by its foraging behavior. As their name implies, flycatchers catch insects on the wing, darting after them from a favorite perch. Most flycatchers sing simple but distinctive songs that help identify them far more effectively than their subdued plumage.

SWIFTS AND SWALLOWS

Members of these two families are typically seen at their nest sites or in flight. Small but sleek, swallows fly gracefully in pursuit of insects. Although swallows are superficially similar to swifts in behavior and appearance, the two groups are not closely related. Swifts are small, dark birds with long, narrow wings and short tails, and they are nearly always seen in flight.

JAYS AND CROWS

Many members of this family can be identified by their intelligence and adaptability. They are easily observed birds that are frequently extremely bold, teasing the animal-human barrier. They are sometimes called 'corvids,' from Corvidae, the scientific name for the family.

SMALL SONGBIRDS

chickadees, wrens, kinglets, etc.
Birds in this group are all generally smaller than a sparrow. Many of them associate with one another in mixed-species flocks. With the exception of the Marsh Wren, most are commonly encountered in city parks, backyards and other wooded areas.

THRUSHES

thrushes, robins, bluebirds
From the robin to the secretive forest thrushes, this group of beautiful singers has the finest collective voice. Although some thrushes are very familiar, others require a little experience and patience to identify.

VIREOS AND WARBLERS

Warblers are splashed liberally with colors, while vireos tend to dress in pale olive. These birds are all very small and sing characteristic courtship songs.

MID-SIZED SONGBIRDS

mockingbirds, waxwings, starlings, etc.
The birds within this group are all sized between a sparrow and a robin. Grosbeaks are very colorful and sing complex flute-like songs, while waxwings are more reserved in dress and voice. Starlings are frequently seen and heard all over San Francisco.

SPARROWS

towhees, sparrows, juncos
These small, often indistinct birds are predominantly brown. Their songs are often very useful in identification. Many birdwatchers discount many of these sparrows as simply 'little brown birds'; this is unfortunate, since these birds are worthy of the extra identification effort. The Spotted Towhee is a colorful exception in the sparrow clan.

BLACKBIRDS

blackbirds, cowbirds, meadowlarks
These birds are predominantly black and have relatively long tails. They are common in open areas, city parks and agricultural fields. Western Meadowlarks belong in the blackbird family despite not being black and having short tails.

FINCHES

finches, goldfinches, siskins, etc.
These finches are year-round residents in San Francisco. They are primarily adapted to feeding on seeds, and they have stout, conical bills. Many are bird-feeder regulars, and they are a familiar part of the winter scene.

ABUNDANCE CHARTS

Accompanying each bird descrip-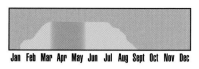
tion is a chart that indicates the
relative abundance of the species
throughout the year. These stylized
graphs offer some insight into the distribution and abundance of the
birds, but they should not be viewed as definitive, as they represent a gen-
eralized overview. There may be inconsistencies specific to time and location, but these charts should provide readers with a basic refernce for bird
abundance and occurrence.

Each chart is divided into the 12 months of the year. The pale orange
that colors the chart is an indication of abundance: the more color, the
more common the bird. Dark orange is used to indicate the nesting
period. As there is little information on breeding dates, the time frame is
approximate, and nesting birds can certainly be found both before and
after the period indicated on the chart. Where no nesting color is shown,
the bird breeds outside the San Francisco area—mainly to the north and
east—and visits San Francisco in significant numbers during migration or
during winter.

These graphs are based on personal observations and on *Birds of Northern
California: An Annotated Field List* (McCaskie et al. 1988).

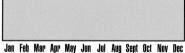

Jan Feb Mar Apr May Jun Jul Aug Sept Oct Nov Dec
abundant

Jan Feb Mar Apr May Jun Jul Aug Sept Oct Nov Dec
common

Jan Feb Mar Apr May Jun Jul Aug Sept Oct Nov Dec
uncommon

Jan Feb Mar Apr May Jun Jul Aug Sept Oct Nov Dec
rare

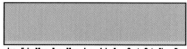

Jan Feb Mar Apr May Jun Jul Aug Sept Oct Nov Dec
unlikely

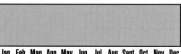

Jan Feb Mar Apr May Jun Jul Aug Sept Oct Nov Dec
absent

BIRDS
S of an Francisco
and the Bay Area

Common Loon
Gavia immer

Jan Feb Mar Apr May Jun Jul Aug Sept Oct Nov Dec

Quick I.D.: goose-sized; stout, sharp bill; sexes similar.
In flight: hunchbacked.
Non-breeding: mottled, gray-brown upperparts; white underparts; light band partway across mid-neck.
Size: 30–34 in.

Loons are highly adapted and therefore restricted to their aquatic lifestyle. To increase their diving ability, they have solid, heavy bones (unlike the hollow bones of chickens and most other birds) and their legs are placed well back on their bodies, but as a result they require long stretches of open water for take-off.

Their intricate dark green (almost black) and white breeding wardrobe gives way to winter browns as many of these birds spend the winter months quietly on San Francisco Bay. Nature lovers can observe loons in the rolling waves at Ocean Beach or Drake's Bay.

Similar Species: Red-throated Loon and Pacific Loon have slimmer bills and lack the light band across their mid-neck; cormorants (pp. 23–25) are generally darker and have longer necks; alcids (pp. 75 & 76) are much smaller.

Pied-billed Grebe
Podilymbus podiceps

The small, stout, drab body of the Pied-billed Grebe seems perfectly suited to its marshy habitat, but its loud, whooping *kuk-kuk-cow-cow-cow-cowp-cowp* is a sound that seems more at home in tropical rainforests.

Pied-billed Grebes can be found on most freshwater wetlands that are surrounded by cattails, bulrushes or other emergent vegetation. These diving birds are frustrating to follow as they disappear and then reappear among the water lilies of urban wetlands. Rodeo Lagoon and Lake Merced usually produce several of these small, reclusive grebes.

Many Pied-billed Grebes remain in the Bay Area during the summer, often nesting within view of lakeside trails. They build nests that float on the water's surface, and their eggs often rest in waterlogged vegetation. Young grebes take their first swim soon after hatching, but they will instinctively clamber aboard a parent's back at the first sign of danger.

Similar Species: Ducks (pp. 32–43) have bills that are flattened top to bottom; Horned Grebe (p. 20) and Eared Grebe have light underparts.

Quick I.D.: smaller than a duck; all-brown; sexes similar.
Breeding: dark vertical band on thick, pale bill; black chin.
First-year young (summer/fall): striped brown and white.
Size: 12–14 in.

Jan Feb Mar Apr May Jun Jul Aug Sept Oct Nov Dec

Horned Grebe
Podiceps auritus

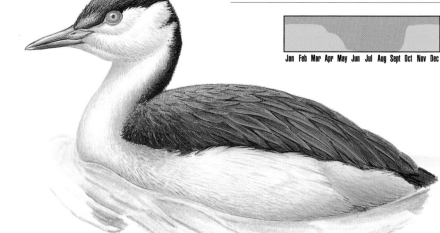

Quick I.D.: smaller than a duck; white cheek; dark crown and upperparts; light underparts; short bill (shorter than width of head); red eyes; sexes similar.
Size: 12½–15 in.

Jan Feb Mar Apr May Jun Jul Aug Sept Oct Nov Dec

Like many waterbirds that winter in the San Francisco area, Horned Grebes lose their splendid summer plumage and assume a low-key, gray-and-white coloring. So dramatic is their transformation that from their summer wardrobe (seen briefly in April before their departure) only their blood-red eyes remain.

Horned Grebes are common in protected bays and along ocean coasts from September through April. They are commonly seen on San Francisco Bay and at Ocean Beach. Their behavior is characteristically peppy: they leap up before neatly diving headfirst into the water.

All grebes eat feathers, a seemingly strange habit that frequently causes their digestive systems to become packed. It is thought that this behavior may protect their stomachs from sharp fish bones, and it may also slow the passage of the bones through the digestive system so that more nutrients. The toes of grebes are also unusual: unlike the fully webbed feet of ducks, gulls, cormorants and alcids, grebes' toes are individually lobed.

Similar Species: Eared Grebe is the same size and has dark cheeks; Pied-billed Grebe (p. 19) has dark underparts and is almost always found in freshwater.

Western Grebe
Aechmophorus occidentalis

Coastal residents are fortunate to have unsurpassed concentrations of this winter visitor. If you gaze out on Golden Gate from Fort Point or West Point, or scan the water from Rodeo Beach, you will frequently have brief, intermittent glimpses of these grebes riding the troughs and peaks of the waves.

The distinguished look of the Western Grebe is refined by its formal plumage, ruby eyes, cobra-like head and long bill. Unlike other overwintering grebes, the Western Grebe doesn't change its plumage over the seasons. The Western Grebe is easily identified by its long, graceful neck as it fishes the open waters for small fish, which it pierces with its dagger-like bill.

Similar Species: Clark's Grebe (often encountered at Lake Merced) lacks the black through the eye.

Quick I.D.: duck-sized; very long neck; black upperparts; yellow-green bill; black mask through eye; white underparts; long bill; sexes similar.

Jan Feb Mar Apr May Jun Jul Aug Sept Oct Nov Dec

Size: 23–28 in.

Brown Pelican
Pelecanus occidentalis

Some people find that the long disproportionate bill, deep pouch, great wing span and dumpy body of the Brown Pelican give it a comical appearance. This odd bird marks the changing seasons when it appears on the Bay at Cliff House and at Bird Island in the spring.

Brown Pelicans often hunt in pairs. After spotting a school of fish, the birds wheel about and plunge headfirst in pursuit. They disappear beneath the waves for a few seconds, and then jolt back up to the water's surface like corks.

Similar Species: American White Pelican (common around salt ponds in San Francisco Bay) is all white, and it has black primaries and a dark orange bill.

Jan Feb Mar Apr May Jun Jul Aug Sept Oct Nov Dec

Quick I.D.: very large; grayish-brown body; gray bill; yellow head; dark belly; sexes similar.
Size: 48 in.

Double-crested Cormorant
Phalacrocorax auritus

The Double-crested Cormorant is a common sight on the West Coast. Like Pelagic and Brandt's cormorants, Double-crests fly in single-file, low over San Francisco Bay. At Lake Merced and inland lakes, however, only Double-crests are seen.

Cormorants lack the ability to waterproof their wings, so they need to dry their wings after each swim. These large black waterbirds are frequently seen perched on seawalls, bridge pilings and buoys, with their wings partially spread to expose their wet feathers to the sun and the wind. It would seem to be a great disadvantage for a waterbird to have to dry its wings, but the cormorant's ability to wet its feathers decreases its buoyancy, making it easier for it to swim after the fish on which it preys. Sealed nostrils, a long, rudder-like tail and excellent underwater vision are other features of the Double-crested Cormorant's aquatic lifestyle.

Similar Species: Brandt's Cormorant (p. 24) is slightly larger, it flies with its neck outstretched, and it has a relatively short tail; Pelagic Cormorant (p. 25) is smaller, it flies with a straight neck, it is iridescent dark green in bright light, and in breeding plumage it has white saddle patches and a red throat pouch; non-breeding loons (p. 18) and large, dark ducks and geese generally have shorter necks and are more stout over-all.

Quick I.D.: goose-sized; all-black; long tail; long neck; sexes similar.
In flight: kinked neck; rapid wingbeats.
Breeding: bright orange throat pouch; black or white plumes streaming back from eyebrows (seen only at close range).
First-year: brown; pale neck, breast and belly.
Size: 30–35 in.

Jan Feb Mar Apr May Jun Jul Aug Sept Oct Nov Dec

Brandt's Cormorant
Phalacrocorax penicillatus

The irregular, long lines of flocks of low-flying Brandt's Cormorants are frequently seen off Ocean Beach. These common birds do not maintain the tight flocks of other species; instead their loose lines mirror the peaks and troughs of the waters over which they fly. They are most frequently encountered within a few miles of the seashore; they tend not to travel over great expanses of open water, except in migration.

The Brandt's Cormorant is the most abundant cormorant in California. On average, 16,000 Brandt's Cormorants nest on the nearby Farallon Islands each year. They nest in colonies atop flat rocks on cliffs, at close but well-maintained distances from one another. They are not normally found on inland waters: only rich salmon runs will periodically persuade these marine birds to feast in freshwater.

Similar Species: Double-crested Cormorant (p. 23) has a proportionally larger head and a pale bill; Pelagic Cormorant (p. 25) is smaller, with a proportionally smaller head and a thinner neck and bill, and it sports white saddle patches in the breeding season.

Quick I.D.: goose-sized; dark over-all; light chin strap; long tail; sexes similar.
In flight: outstretched neck.
Breeding: blue throat pouch, fine white plumes on neck and back.
First-year: dark brown upperparts; pale underparts.
Size: 28–33 in.

Jan Feb Mar Apr May Jun Jul Aug Sept Oct Nov Dec

Pelagic Cormorant
Phalacrocorax pelagicus

The all-black Pelagic Cormorant is the smallest and slimmest cormorant of the West Coast. It nests precariously on thin cliff ledges, laying its eggs in a meager nest of seaweed and guano. Cormorant colonies are not found very close to San Francisco because they are sensitive to human disturbances.

Like their close relatives the pelicans, cormorants have a naked throat pouch and fully webbed feet (all four toes are linked with webbing). Cormorants overheat easily and they are frequently seen with their bills open during hot weather, panting to cool off.

In San Francisco, the Pelagic Cormorant can best be observed from Fort Point or Lincoln Park. The Double-crested Cormorant is also common; to identify the Pelagic, look for the cormorant that holds its neck straight out in flight and sports two white saddle patches during the breeding season (late winter to early summer).

Similar Species: Double-crested Cormorant (p. 23) is larger, and its neck is kinked in flight; Brandt's Cormorant (p. 24) is larger, it flies with its neck outstretched and its has a relatively short tail; non-breeding loons (p. 18) and large, dark ducks and geese generally have shorter necks and are more stout over-all.

Quick I.D.: smaller than a goose; sleek, dark plumage; long tail; small head; sexes similar.
In flight: straight neck.
Breeding: white saddle patches; inconspicuous, red throat pouch.
Size: 25–28 in.

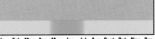

Jan Feb Mar Apr May Jun Jul Aug Sept Oct Nov Dec

Great Blue Heron
Ardea herodias

The Great Blue Heron is one of the largest and most regal of the coastal birds. It often stands motionless as it surveys the calm waters, its graceful lines blending naturally with the grasses and cattails of inland wetlands. All herons have specialized vertebrae that enable the neck to fold back over itself. The S-shaped neck, seen in flight, identifies all members of this wading family.

Hunting herons space themselves out evenly in favorite hunting spots, and they will strike out suddenly at prey below the water's surface. In flight, their lazy wingbeats slowly but effortlessly carry them up to their nests. These herons nest communally high in trees, building bulky stick nests that are sometimes in plain sight of urban areas.

The shallows of San Francisco Bay, Lake Merritt, Bolinas Lagoon and other, smaller wetlands often produce great numbers of this fascinating year-round resident.

Similar Species: None.

Quick I.D.: very large heron; eagle-sized wingspan; gray-blue plumage; red thighs; long, dagger-like, yellow bill; sexes similar.
In flight: head folded back; legs held straight back.
Size: 42–50 in.

Jan Feb Mar Apr May Jun Jul Aug Sept Oct Nov Dec

Black-crowned Night-Heron
Nycticorax nycticorax

Quick I.D.: mid-sized heron; black crown and back; gray neck and wings; white cheek and belly; moderately long legs; sexes similar.
Breeding: white plumes from back of head.
Juvenile: brown; heavily streaked and spotted.
Size: 28 in.

Jan Feb Mar Apr May Jun Jul Aug Sept Oct Nov Dec

Alcatraz is best-known for its past use as a prison, but it is also a great spot to watch Black-crowned Night-Herons. These stocky, colorful herons are widespread in the Bay Area, but those roosting and nesting on Alcatraz are acclimatized to humans and will tolerate closer contact.

Black-crowned Night-Herons forage in estuaries, tidal flats, lagoons and freshwater ponds just before sunrise and sunset. They are more difficult to find in the middle of the day. As daylight fades over a flock of foraging night-herons, their characteristic *wok-wok* call continues to be imprinted in the mind long after their silhouettes have disappeared into the night.

Similar Species: Great Blue Heron (p. 26) is larger and has a long neck; Green Heron has a greenish-black cap, a chestnut neck and greenish upperparts; American Bittern is similar to a juvenile night-heron, but it has black wingtips and a black mustache stripe.

Great Egret
Ardea alba

The silky silhouette of the Great Egret graces many marshes, tidal flats and estuaries in the Bay Area. It stalks shallow waters for fish, amphibians and sometimes small birds and mammals. The diligence and patience it displays while hunting contrasts with its lightning-quick, spearing thrust. At dusk, waves of these ghostly birds trace their way back to their communal nesting and roosting sites, which are usually in areas isolated from humans. Nesting can be viewed at Audubon Canyon Ranch on Bolinas Lagoon.

From January through late spring, the Great Egret's form is enhanced by the presence of 'nuptial plumes' that flare from its lower neck. Earlier this century, people coveted these feathers for fashion accessories, and Great Egret populations were decimated before legislation was enacted to protect them.

Similar Species: Snowy Egret (p. 29) is smaller and has yellow feet.

Quick I.D.: large heron; all-white plumage; long, yellow bill; black legs and feet; sexes similar. *Breeding:* long white plumes from back and base of neck; green lores.
Size: 38 in.

Jan Feb Mar Apr May Jun Jul Aug Sept Oct Nov Dec

Snowy Egret
Egretta thula

While all other herons and egrets hunting the shallows in San Francisco Bay do so in slow, purposeful strides, the Snowy Egret chooses a more energetic approach. It stirs the water with its golden slippers—its black legs are tipped with bright yellow toes that glow in the shallow tidal pools and marshes—to lure small fish, crustaceans and insects into striking range. Should this egret not succeed in its foot-waving foray, it may extend a wing over the open pool to trick fish into swimming towards the shade. Once its prey is within range, the Snowy Egret plucks it from the false haven with the accuracy characteristic of all herons.

Of all the long-legged waders in the Bay Area, the Snowy Egret may be the most social nester. Its shallow stick platform is frequently built low in trees. These nesting colonies are vulnerable to human disturbance, and you should keep a respectful distance from them. Safe viewing of nesting is possible at Lake Merritt in Oakland.

Similar Species: Great Egret (p. 28) is larger and has black feet; Black-crowned Night-heron (p. 27) has a black cap and back, a gray neck and gray wings; Cattle Egret has a yellow bill and is smaller.

Quick I.D.: mid-sized heron; all-white plumage; black bill and legs; yellow feet; yellow lores; sexes similar.
Size: 23 in.

Jan Feb Mar Apr May Jun Jul Aug Sept Oct Nov Dec

American Coot
Fulica americana

The American Coot has the lobed toes of a grebe, the bill of a chicken and the body shape and swimming habits of a duck, but it is not remotely related to any of these species: its closest cousins are rails and cranes. American Coots dabble and dive in water and forage on land, and they eat both plant and animal matter. They can be found in just about every freshwater pond, lake, marsh, lagoon or city park in San Francisco. They are inland breeders that retreat in great numbers to our mild coastal climates for the winter.

These loud, grouchy birds are seen chugging along in wetlands, frequently entering into short-lived disputes with other coots. American Coots appear comical while they swim: their heads bob in time with their paddling feet, and as a coot's swimming speed increases, so does the back-and-forth motion of its head. At peak speed, this motion seems to disorient the coot, and it will run, flap and splash towards the other side of the wetland.

Similar Species: All ducks (pp. 32–43) and grebes (pp. 19–21) generally lack the uniform black color and the white bill.

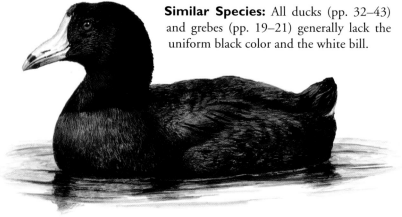

Jan Feb Mar Apr May Jun Jul Aug Sept Oct Nov Dec

Quick I.D.: smaller than a duck; black body; white bill; red forehead shield; short tail; long legs; lobed feet; white undertail coverts; sexes similar.
Size: 15 in.

Canada Goose
Branta canadensis

Most flocks of Canada Geese in city parks and golf courses show little concern for their human neighbors. These urban geese seem to think nothing of creating a traffic jam, blocking a fairway or dining on lawns and gardens.

Breeding pairs mate for life, and not only will a widowed goose occasionally remain unpaired for the rest of its life, it's common for a mate to stay at the side of a fallen partner. Canada Geese are common along the east shore of San Francisco Bay and at Lake Merritt in Oakland. Many subspecies migrate through northwestern California, and they can be recognized by differences in size and color. Most Canada Geese seen around San Francisco are of the large race from the Great Basin in eastern California. These pale-breasted birds were likely introduced into Lake Merritt, where they have since established a large, year-round breeding population.

Similar Species: Brant and large dabbling ducks are smaller and lack the white cheek; Greater White-fronted Goose lacks the white cheek and the black head and neck.

Quick I.D.: large goose; white cheek; black head and neck; brown body; white undertail coverts; sexes similar.
Size: 35–43 in.

Jan Feb Mar Apr May Jun Jul Aug Sept Oct Nov Dec

Mallard
Anas platyrhynchos

The Mallard is the classic duck of inland marshes—the male's iridescent green head and chestnut breast are symbolic of wetland habitat. This large duck is commonly seen feeding in city parks, small lakes and shallow bays. With their legs positioned under the middle part of their bodies, Mallards walk easily, and they can spring straight out of water without a running start.

Mallards are the most common duck in North America (and the Northern Hemisphere), and they are easily seen year-round in San Francisco. During the winter, flocks of Mallards are seen in open freshwater or grazing along shorelines. Because several species often band together in these loose flocks, birdwatchers habitually scan these groups to test their identification skills. Mallards (like all ducks) molt several times a year, so remember that the distinctive green head of the male Mallards occasionally loses its green pizzazz.

Similar Species: Male Northern Shoveler (p. 34) has a green head, a white breast and chestnut flanks; female Mallard resembles many other female dabbling ducks, but look for the blue speculum and her close association with the males.

Quick I.D.: large duck; bright orange feet. *Male:* iridescent green head; bright yellow bill; chestnut breast; white flanks. *Female:* mottled brown; blue speculum bordered by white; bright orange bill marked with black.

Jan Feb Mar Apr May Jun Jul Aug Sept Oct Nov Dec **Size:** 22–26 in.

Northern Pintail
Anas acuta

The Northern Pintail is the most elegant duck to be found along the shores of San Francisco Bay. The male's long tapering tail feathers and graceful neck contribute to the sleek appearance of this handsome bird. As winter frosts bear down upon northern lands, Northern Pintails are driven to the Bay Area to escape the freeze-up. By late November, they have arrived in peak numbers, and they are the most abundant waterfowl in the state. During this time of year, pintails are encountered on lakes, saltwater bays, estuaries and tidal channels, characteristically 'tipping up' and extending their graceful tails skywards.

Northern Pintails breed in small numbers in the Bay Area. The hidden nest sites are often great distances from freshwater marshes and lakes. When the ducklings hatch, the hens may have to march the downy young over a mile to the sanctuary of a wetland.

Similar Species: Mallard (p. 32), American Wigeon (p 35) and Gadwall are all chunkier and lack the tapered tail.

Quick I.D.: large duck; long, slender neck; long, tapered tail; bluish bill.
In flight: appears slender and sleek.
Male: chocolate-brown head; very long tail; white breast extending up base of neck; dusty gray body.
Female: mottled light-brown over-all.
Size: *Male:* 26–30 in.
Female: 21–23 in.

Jan Feb Mar Apr May Jun Jul Aug Sept Oct Nov Dec

Northern Shoveler
Anas clypeata

The Northern Shoveler's shovel-like bill stands out among dabbling ducks. Its species name—*clypeata*—is Latin for 'furnished with a shield.' The comb-like structures along the bill's edges and its broad, flat shape allow the shoveler to strain small plants and invertebrates from the water's surface or from muddy substrates. A few Northern Shovelers breed in the Bay Area, but most of the shovelers seen in the winter reproduce far inland.

Many novice birders become interested in birds because they realize the great variety of ducks in their city parks. Some ducks, like the Northern Shoveler, are dabblers that prefer shallow water, that are not opposed to roaming around on land and that lift straight off the water like a helicopter. Many other ducks in the San Francisco area are divers that are found on large lakes and saltwater bays. They can be seen running across the water to gain enough speed for flight. Separating the divers from the dabblers is a first step into the wondrous world of waterfowl.

Similar Species: Mallard (p. 32) and all other dabbling ducks lack the combination of a large bill, a white breast and chestnut sides.

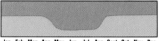

Jan Feb Mar Apr May Jun Jul Aug Sept Oct Nov Dec

Quick I.D: mid-sized duck; large bill (longer than head width).
Male: green head; white breast; chestnut sides.
Female: mottled brown over-all.
Size: 18–20 in.

American Wigeon
Anas americana

Quick I.D.: mid-sized duck; cinnamon breast and flanks; white belly; gray bill with black tip; green speculum.
Male: white forehead; green swipe running back from eye.
Female: lacks distinct color on head.
Size: 18–21 in.

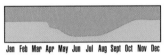

Jan Feb Mar Apr May Jun Jul Aug Sept Oct Nov Dec

During the winter, American Wigeons can easily be found and identified in the shallows and grassy shorelines of San Francisco's ponds. From mid-October through April, flocks of widgeons waddle across lawns in Golden Gate Park, begging scraps intended for pigeons. The white top and gray sides of the male American Wigeon's head look somewhat like a balding scalp, while the nasal *wee-he-he-he* calls sound remarkably like the squeaks of a squeezed rubber ducky.

Flocks of American Widgeons, one of our most common North American dabblers, occasionally include some Eurasian Wigeons, their Siberian counterpart. Hundreds of these Asian birds take a wrong turn at the Bering Sea each year and accidentally follow the American shoreline instead of the Asian one during their fall migration.

Similar Species: Eurasian Wigeon (breeds in Asia) has a gold forehead and a cinnamon head without a green swipe; Green-winged Teal is smaller, it has a white shoulder slash, and it has a rusty head with a green swipe.

Canvasback
Aythya valisineria

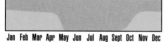

Jan Feb Mar Apr May Jun Jul Aug Sept Oct Nov Dec

Quick I.D.: mid-sized duck; sloping bill and forehead.
Male: canvas-white back; chestnut head; black breast and hindquarters.
Female: brown head and neck; lighter body.
Size: 19–23 in.

At Lake Merritt during the winter, scores of these white-backed ducks swim majestically with their bills held high. Canvasbacks are ducks of the deep freshwater, and they acquire their vegetarian diet in well-spaced dives. Although birders can easily identify the stately Canvasback at a distance, one can closely study the duck's ruby eyes and rich mahogany head each day during the breeding season at Lake Merritt. The Canvasback's distinctive profile results from the apparent lack of a forehead. The dark bill appears to run straight up to the top of the bird's head, giving the Canvasback sleek, hydrodynamic-looking contours.

Redheads are quite rare in San Francisco, but they are noteworthy in comparison to Canvasbacks. Like the male Canvasback, the male Redhead's head is ... red, but its back is gray. Also, the Redhead has a noticeable forehead, just like that of a scaup.

Similar Species: Lesser Scaup (p. 38) and Greater Scaup lack the chestnut head and the sloping forehead; Redhead lacks the sloping forehead and has a black-tipped bill and a darker back.

Ring-necked Duck
Aythya collaris

From late September to mid-April, Ring-necked Ducks overwinter on wooded ponds and lakes in Golden Gate Park and on Rodeo Lagoon. These diving ducks prefer ponds and lakes with muddy bottoms; they dive deeply underwater for aquatic vegetation, including seeds, tubers and pondweed leaves, and for aquatic invertebrates. Because of their foraging habits, Ring-necked Ducks are susceptible to poisoning from ingesting lead shot: wasted shotgun pellets lie at the bottom of many rural wetlands and throughout this duck's summer range across the northern states and Canada.

Although this duck's name implies the presence of a collar, most experienced birders have given up on seeing this faint feature. The only prominent ring noticeable in field observations is around the tip of the bill, suggesting that a more reasonable name for this bird would have been 'Ring-billed Duck.'

Similar Species: Lesser Scaup (p. 38) and Greater Scaup lack the white shoulder slash and the black back; female Redhead has a dark brown head to match its body.

Quick I.D.: mid-sized duck; black bill tip; white bill ring.
Male: dark head with hints of purple; black breast, back and hindquarters; white shoulder slash; gray sides; of bill; blue-gray bill with black and white banding at tip and prominent white ring around base.
Female: dark brown body; light brown head; white eye-ring; lighter color closer to bill.
Size: 17 in.

Jan Feb Mar Apr May Jun Jul Aug Sept Oct Nov Dec

Lesser Scaup
Aythya affinis

The Lesser Scaup is the Oreo cookie of the coastal ducks—black at both ends and white in the middle. It is a diving duck that prefers deep, open water, and it is common on lakes, harbors, estuaries and lagoons. As a result of its diving adaptations, the Lesser Scaup is clumsy on land and during take-off, but it gains dignity when it takes to the water. For close-up views, visit the duck-feeding area at Lake Merritt in Oakland.

Because of San Francisco's coastal location, most species of ducks here are of the diving variety, even though the dabblers are often the most frequently encountered. Diving ducks have smaller wings, which helps them dive underwater but makes for difficult take-offs and landings. When a duck scoots across the water in an attempt to get airborne, even a first-time birder can tell it's a diver. Divers' legs are placed well back on their bodies—an advantage for underwater swimming—so in order for diving ducks to stand, they must raise their heavy front ends high to maintain balance.

Similar Species: Greater Scaup has a green tinge to its head and a long white stripe on the trailing edge of its wing (seen in flight), and its head is more rounded; Ring-necked Duck (p. 37) has a white shoulder slash and a black back.

Jan Feb Mar Apr May Jun Jul Aug Sept Oct Nov Dec

Quick I.D.: peaked head.
Male: dark head with hints of purple; black breast and hindquarters; sides dirty white; back grayish; bill blue-gray; no white shoulder slash.
Female: dark brown; well-defined white patch at base of bill.
Size: 15–17 in.

Surf Scoter
Melanitta perspicillata

Quick I.D.: large duck.
Male: black over-all; white forehead, nape and base of bill; orange bill.
Female: dark brown; light cheek.
Size: 18–21 in.

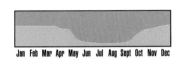

Jan Feb Mar Apr May Jun Jul Aug Sept Oct Nov Dec

Tough, big and stocky, scoters are more strong than graceful. They are deep-diving sea ducks, and stormy weather amounts to nothing more than a simple annoyance in their feeding habits. Surf Scoters are frequently observed among white-capped waves, and on choppy seas they live up to their name by 'scooting' across the water's surface, occasionally crashing through incoming waves.

Surf Scoters form rafts in San Francisco Bay during the winter months. They dive to wrench shellfish from rocks with their sturdy bills, and they swallow the shellfish whole. In the spring, these large black ducks migrate to lakes and tundra ponds as far north as Alaska and the Yukon.

Similar Species: White-winged Scoter has white wing patches, and the male has a white eye spot; male Black Scoter is all-black; female Black Scoter has a white face and throat; other dark waterfowl lack the white forehead and nape.

Common Goldeneye
Bucephala clangula

Quick I.D.: mid-sized duck.
Male: large, dark green to black head; round, white cheek patch; white body; black back streaked with white.
Female: chocolate-brown hood; sandy-colored body.

Jan Feb Mar Apr May Jun Jul Aug Sept Oct Nov Dec

Size: 17–19 in.

Although Common Goldeneyes don't breed in the San Francisco area, they are locally common from late fall right up to their spring migration. Their courtship antics, staged on San Francisco Bay, Lake Merritt and just about every other large waterbody from winter through spring, reinforce a pair's bond prior to their migration to Canadian woodland lakes.

The courtship display of this widespread duck is one of nature's best slapstick routines. The spry male goldeneye rapidly arches his large green head back until his bill points skyward, producing a seemingly painful *kraaaagh*. Completely unaffected by this chiropractic wonder, he continuously performs this ritual to mainly disinterested females. The male continually escalates his spring performance, creating a comedic scene that is most appreciated by birdwatchers.

Similar Species: Hooded Merganser, Bufflehead (p. 41) and Barrow's Goldeneye all lack the round, white cheek patch.

Bufflehead
Bucephala albeola

Quick I.D.: tiny duck; round body.
Male: white triangle on back of dark head;
white body; dark back.
Female: dirty brown; small white cheek
patch.
Size: 13–15 in.

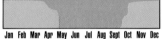

Jan Feb Mar Apr May Jun Jul Aug Sept Oct Nov Dec

The small, fluffy Bufflehead is perhaps the 'cutest' of San Francisco's ducks: their simple plumage and rotund physique bring to mind a child's stuffed toy. During the winter, they are found on just about every lake, pond and wetland in the area. Although common in parks and urban ponds, Buffleheads (unlike many other duck species) rarely accept handouts from humans.

Because ducks spend most of their lives dripping with water, preening is an important behavior. At the base of the tail of most birds lies the preen (uropygial) gland, which secretes a viscous liquid that inhibits bacterial growth, and waterproofs and conditions the feathers. After gently squeezing the preen gland with its bill, a bird can spread the secretion methodically over most of its body, an essential practice to revitalize precious feathers. Since sun and wind damage feathers, it is understandable that birds spend so much time preening and conditioning their feathers.

Similar Species: Males of Common Goldeneye (p. 40), Barrow's Goldeneye and Hooded Merganser are all larger and lack the white, unbordered triangle behind the eye.

Red-breasted Merganser
Mergus serrator

The Red-breasted Merganser runs along the surface of the water, beating its heavy wings, to build up sufficient speed for lift-off. Once in the air, this large duck looks compressed and arrow-like as it flies strongly in low, straight lines. Mergansers are lean and powerful waterfowl adapted to the underwater pursuit of fish. Unlike other fishing birds, a merganser has a saw-like bill that is serrated to ensure that squirmy, slimy prey do not escape.

Red-breasted Mergansers are found almost exclusively on saltwater in the San Francisco area during the winter. Their quick 'fly bys' and flashing, white inner wing patches are common winter features off Ocean Beach and Point Bonita.

Similar Species: Male Common Merganser (rare in San Francisco) lacks the red breast and has white underparts; female Common Merganser has a well-defined, reddish-brown hood; other large ducks and Common Loon (p. 18) all lack the combination of a green head, an orange bill, orange feet and a red breast.

Jan Feb Mar Apr May Jun Jul Aug Sept Oct Nov Dec

Quick I.D.: large duck; gray body.
Male: well-defined, dark green hood; punk-like crest; spotted, red breast; white collar; brilliant orange bill and feet; black spinal streak.
Female: rusty hood blending into white chest.
Size: 21–25 in.

Ruddy Duck
Oxyura jamaicensis

Quick I.D.: small duck; broad bill; large head; tail often cocked up.
Breeding male: reddish-brown neck and body; black head and tail; white cheek; blue bill.
Non-breeding male: dull brown over-all; dark cap; white cheek.
Female: like non-breeding male, but pale cheek has a dark stripe.
Size: 14–16 in.

Jan Feb Mar Apr May Jun Jul Aug Sept Oct Nov Dec

The clowns of freshwater wetlands, male Ruddy Ducks energetically paddle around their breeding wetlands, displaying with great vigor and beating their breasts with their bright blue beaks. The *plap-plap-plap-plap-plap* sound of their display speeds up until its climax: a spasmodic jerk and sputter. The male's performance occurs from May to the middle of June and can be seen at Lake Merced.

The Ruddy Duck's winter demeanor contrasts sharply with its summer habits. The drably plumaged males lack their courting energy and their summer colors. These stiff-tailed diving ducks are found commonly during the non-breeding season offshore on San Francisco Bay and Rodeo Lagoon.

Similar Species: All other waterfowl are generally larger and have shorter tails and relatively smaller heads.

Osprey
Pandion haliaetus

The Osprey is commonly seen over large waterbodies from April through September. A number of nesting sites occur near the San Francisco area, and a short drive north to Tomales Bay will provide an opportunity to observe these large raptors nesting on abandoned duck blinds.

To hunt, an Osprey surveys the calm water of a coastal bay from the air. Spotting a flash of silver at the water's surface, the Osprey folds its great wings and dives towards the fish. An instant before striking the water, the bird thrusts its talons forward to grasp its slippery prey. The Osprey may completely disappear beneath the water to ensure a successful capture; then it reappears, slapping its wings on the surface as it returns to the air. Once it has regained flight, the Osprey shakes off the residual water and heads off toward its bulky stick nest, holding its prey facing forward.

Similar Species: Bald Eagle is larger and never has the combination of white underparts and a white head with an eye streak; other large raptors are seldom seen near water; gulls (pp. 68–72) are smaller and have more pointed wings.

Quick I.D.: larger than a hawk; white underparts; dark elbow patches; white head; dark streak through eye; sexes similar.
In flight: wings held in a shallow 'M.'
Size: 21–24 in.

Jan Feb Mar Apr May Jun Jul Aug Sept Oct Nov Dec

Turkey Vulture
Cathartes aura

Soaring effortlessly above the Marin Headlands, Turkey Vultures ride rising thermals during their afternoon foraging flights. They seldom need to flap their silver-lined wings, and they rock gently from side to side as they carefully scan fields and shorelines for carcasses. Even at great distances, this bare-headed bird can be identified by the way it tends to hold its wings upwards in a shallow 'V.'

The Turkey Vulture feeds entirely on carrion, which it can sometimes detect by scent alone. Its head is featherless, which is an adaptation to staying clean and parasite-free while it digs around inside carcasses. The Turkey Vulture's well-known habit of regurgitating its rotting meal at intruders may be a defense mechanism: it allows adults to reduce their weight for quicker take-off, and its smell helps young vultures repel would-be predators.

Similar Species: Hawks (pp. 47–50), eagles and Osprey (p. 44) all have large, feathered heads and tend to hold their wings flatter in flight, not in a shallow 'V.'

Quick I.D.: larger than a hawk; all-black; small red head; sexes similar.
In flight: wings held in a shallow 'V'; silver-gray flight feathers; dark wing linings.
Size: 27 in.

Jan Feb Mar Apr May Jun Jul Aug Sept Oct Nov Dec

White-tailed Kite
Elanus leucurus

The White-tailed Kite flies with unusual grace and buoyancy for a raptor. It normally hunts during dawn and dusk, when it can be found hovering over rolling hills, wet meadows and cultivated fields. The population of this regal bird (formerly known as the Black-shouldered Kite) appears to have stabilized recently, after serious declines caused by egg collectors, habitat loss and unwarranted shootings.

The White-tailed Kite nests in trees and tall bushes in semi-open areas. The nests are often built near the treetop, away from the main trunk and horizontal limbs. During incubation and after hatching, the male kite diligently provides the growing family with steady feasts of small rodents, which he catches in prime habitats near the nest. When the White-tailed Kite spots a vole wandering through the grass, it parachutes down on the rodent, with its wings held high.

Similar Species: Falcons (pp. 51 & 52) and hawks (pp. 47–50) lack the pure-white tail and black shoulders; male Northern Harrier (p. 47) lacks the black shoulders and has a conspicuous white rump.

Quick I.D.:
small hawk–sized; long white tail; pointed wings; black shoulders; gray back; sexes similar. *In flight:* frequently hovers.
Size: 16 in.

Jan Feb Mar Apr May Jun Jul Aug Sept Oct Nov Dec

Northern Harrier
Circus cyaneus

This common marsh hawk can best be identified by its flight behavior: the Northern Harrier traces wavy lines over lush meadows, often retracing its path several times in the quest for prey. Watch the slow, lazy wingbeats of the Northern Harrier coincide with its undulating, erratic flight pattern as this raptor skims the brambles and bulrushes with its belly. Unlike other hawks, which can find their prey only visually, the Northern Harrier stays close enough to the ground to listen for birds, voles and mice. When movement catches the Harrier's eyes or ears, it abandons its lazy ways to strike at prey with channeled energy.

The purposeful, low, coursing flights can occasionally be observed over Rodeo Lagoon during July and August, as juveniles disperse from their nest sites. A few pairs of Northern Harriers continue to breed near San Francisco at Point Reyes and Año Nuevo.

Similar Species: Short-eared Owl and Sharp-shinned (p. 48), Red-tailed (p. 49) and Cooper's hawks all lack the white rump.

Quick I.D.: mid-sized hawk; white rump; long tail; long wings; owl-like face (seen only at close range).
Male: grayish upperparts; whitish underparts; black wingtips.
Female and *Immature:* brown over-all.
Size: 20 in.

Jan Feb Mar Apr May Jun Jul Aug Sept Oct Nov Dec

HAWKS AND FALCONS 47

Sharp-shinned Hawk
Accipiter striatus

If songbirds dream, the Sharp-shinned Hawk is sure to be the source of their nightmares. 'Sharpies' pursue small birds through forests, passing by limbs and branches in the hope of acquiring prey. Sharp-shinned Hawks take more birds than other accipiters, with small songbirds and the occasional woodpecker being the most numerous items. These small hawks are easy to find at Hawk Hill as they pass through the Marin Headlands during their fall migration. During the winter months, many of San Francisco's wooded neighborhoods have a resident Sharp-shinned Hawk, eager to capture unwary finches, sparrows and starlings.

Sharp-shinned Hawks terrorize the songbirds living in San Francisco's neighborhoods. Backyard feeders tend to concentrate sparrows and finches, so they are attractive foraging areas for this small hawk. A sudden eruption of songbirds off the feeder and a few feathers floating on the wind are often the signs of a sudden, successful Sharp-shinned attack.

Similar Species: Cooper's Hawk is usually larger, and its tail is rounded and has a wide terminal band; Merlin has pointed wings and rapid wingbeats, and it lacks the red chest streaks; Red-shouldered Hawk (p. 50) is larger and has wider tail bands.

Quick I.D.: pigeon-sized; short, round wings; long tail; blue-gray back; red horizontal streaking on underparts; red eyes.
In flight: flap-and-glide flier; heavily barred tail is straight at the end.
Immature: brown over-all; vertical, brown streaks on chest; yellow eyes.
Size: 12–14 in. (female larger).

Jan Feb Mar Apr May Jun Jul Aug Sept Oct Nov Dec

Red-tailed Hawk
Buteo jamaicensis

With its fierce facial expression and untidy feathers, the Red-tailed Hawk looks as though it has been suddenly and rudely awakened. Its characteristic scream further suggests that the Red-tailed Hawk is a bird best avoided. You would think other birds would treat this large raptor with more respect, but the Red-tailed Hawk is constantly being harassed by crows, jays and blackbirds.

It isn't until this hawk is two or three years old that its tail becomes brick red. The dark head, black 'belt' around its midsection and the dark leading edge to its wings are better field marks because they're seen in most Red-tails. Where Highway 1 passes through open country south of San Francisco, it's hard not to spot a Red-tail perched on a post or soaring lazily overhead.

Similar Species: Northern Harrier (p. 47) has a white rump; Sharp-shinned Hawk (p. 48) and Cooper's Hawk are smaller, have long tails and rarely soar; Red-shouldered Hawk (p. 50) is smaller and has broad, dark tail bands; Rough-legged Hawk (rare winter migrant) has distinctive elbow patches.

Quick I.D.: large hawk; brick-red tail (adult only); dark head; thin brown belt; light flight feathers; dark wing lining; sexes similar.
Size: 22 in.

Jan Feb Mar Apr May Jun Jul Aug Sept Oct Nov Dec

Red-shouldered Hawk
Buteo lineatus

Unlike many other hawks in the Bay Area, the Red-shouldered Hawk does most of its hunting from a perch. Sitting atop a fencepost, utility pole or tree, this small, intricately colored raptor waits patiently above a lake or wet meadow. From its vantage point, it uses keen eyes and sharp ears to detect frogs, toads, snakes, mice and occasionally crayfish or other invertebrates.

The Red-shouldered Hawk nests in mature trees, usually near water, and the stick nest is built in a crotch. Look for them around lakes in Golden Gate Park or at Lake Merced. As spring approaches and pair bonds are formed and reinforced, the normally docile hawks utter loud and shrieking *kee-you kee-you kee-you* calls.

Similar Species: Red-tailed Hawk (p. 49) is larger and lacks the tail banding; Sharp-shinned Hawk (p. 48) and Cooper's Hawk have longer, narrower tails and lack the rufous shoulders.

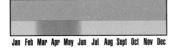

Jan Feb Mar Apr May Jun Jul Aug Sept Oct Nov Dec

Quick I.D.: mid-sized hawk; heavily banded tail; red wing linings; dark rufous chest with white, horizontal streaks; sexes similar.
Size: 19 in.

American Kestrel
Falco sparverius

This small, noisy falcon is a common summer sight over much of California. It has adapted well to rural life, and it is commonly seen perched on power lines, watching for unwary grasshoppers, birds and rodents. When not perched, American Kestrels can often be seen hovering above potential prey. All falcons are skilled hunters, and they have a unique, tooth-like projection on their hooked bills that can quickly crush the neck of small prey. The American Kestrel's species name *sparverius* is Latin for 'pertaining to sparrows,' an occasional prey item.

The nests of American Kestrels are often built in abandoned woodpecker cavities. Conservationists have recently discovered that kestrels will use nest boxes when natural cavities are unavailable, which should ensure that these active predators remain common throughout the San Francisco area.

Similar Species: Sharp-shinned Hawk (p. 48) and Cooper's Hawk have short, rounder wings; Merlin is larger, has a banded tail and lacks the facial stripes.

Quick I.D.: jay-sized; long, pointed wings; long tail; two vertical, black stripes on face; spotted breast; hooked bill.
In flight: rapid wingbeat.
Male: blue wings; russet back; colorful head.
Female: russet back and wings.
Size: 11 in.

Jan Feb Mar Apr May Jun Jul Aug Sept Oct Nov Dec

Peregrine Falcon
Falco peregrinus

The Peregrine Falcon is one of the fastest animals in the world, and it can reach speeds of up to 100 mph. Once a Peregrine has its prey singled out, even the fastest ducks and shorebirds have little chance of escaping this effective predator. The Peregrine Falcon plunges on its prey, punching large birds in mid-air and following them to the ground, where they are killed and eaten.

California's Peregrines declined to near extinction because of pesticide residues in the environment. An active recovery plan for this endangered species has restored the population, and this magnificent bird can now be found breeding on skyscrapers and bridges around San Francisco. Along the wild, rocky shorelines, a few pairs breed, delighting and astonishing those who view their extraordinary hunting skills.

Similar Species: Prairie Falcon (rare in San Francisco) has black 'wing pits'; Merlin and American Kestrel (p. 51) are much smaller.

Jan Feb Mar Apr May Jun Jul Aug Sept Oct Nov Dec

Quick I.D.: crow-sized; dark blue hood extending down cheek; steel-blue upperparts; light underparts with dark speckles.
In flight: pointed wings; long tail.
Immature: like adults except brown where adults are steel-blue; more heavily streaked underparts.
Size: 15–20 in.

California Quail
Callipepla californica

With its distinctive forward-facing plume, the California Quail looks like a flapper from the 1920s. California Quail scuttle around in tight, cohesive groups, and in the fall and winter, these coveys can include up to 200 birds.

In most of San Francisco's large parks, coveys have succumbed to predation by released feral cats, but in the Marin Headlands they are still often seen darting across paths in search of dense cover. Even when these shy birds refuse to leave their shrubby sanctuary, their noisy scratching and soft vocalizations betray their presence. During April and May, listen as the males advertise their courting desires by characteristically uttering *where are you?*

Similar Species: None.

Quick I.D.: robin-sized; forward-facing plume; gray-brown back; gray chest; white scales on belly; unfeathered legs.
Male: black throat; white stripes on head and neck.
Female: gray-brown face and throat.
Size: 10 in.

Jan Feb Mar Apr May Jun Jul Aug Sept Oct Nov Dec

Killdeer
Charadrius vociferus

The Killdeer is probably the most widespread shorebird in California. It nests on gravely shorelines, utility rights-of-way, lawns, pastures and occasionally on gravel roofs within cities. Its name is a paraphrase of its distinctive, loud call—*kill-dee kill-dee kill-deer.*

The Killdeer's response to predators relies on deception and good acting skills. To divert a predator's attention away from a nest or a brood of young, an adult Killdeer (like many shorebirds) will flop around to feign an injury (usually a broken wing or leg). Once the Killdeer has the attention of the fox, crow or gull, it leads the predator away from the vulnerable nest. After it reaches a safe distance, the adult Killdeer is suddenly 'healed' and flies off, leaving the predator without a meal.

Similar Species: Semipalmated Plover has only one chest band, is smaller and is found only on mudflats.

Jan Feb Mar Apr May Jun Jul Aug Sept Oct Nov Dec

Quick I.D.: robin-sized; two black bands across breast; brown back; russet rump; long legs; white underparts; sexes similar.
Size: 9–11 in.

Black-bellied Plover
Pluvialis squatarola

During the winter, Black-bellied Plovers are commonly seen darting along sea beaches, grassy openings and ploughed fields, foraging with a robin-like run-and-stop technique. Although they dress in plain grays for much of their San Francisco retreat, many Black-bellied Plovers can be seen in their summer tuxedo plumage in early spring and late fall.

Not all walks along Ocean Beach will bring an encounter with a plover, but a keen observer can determine if one was strolling the sand earlier. The Black-bellied Plover lacks a hind digit and leaves a three-toed print, whereas most other sandpipers that overwinter on the coast have four toes.

Similar Species: Willet (p. 64) is larger and has a longer bill; other shorebirds don't use the run-and-stop feeding technique, are not as plump or as gray.

Quick I.D.: larger than a robin; short, stout, black bill; relatively long, dark legs; sexes similar.
Non-breeding: slightly streaked, gray body.
In flight: black wing pits; white rump; white wing linings.
Size: 12 in.

Jan Feb Mar Apr May Jun Jul Aug Sept Oct Nov Dec

Black Turnstone
Arenaria melanocephala

During migration and in the winter, Black Turnstones live on barnacle-and seaweed-covered rocky outcrops. They can often be seen in rocky areas near the Sutro Baths or on reefs, breakwaters and rocky beaches throughout our region. Turnstones probe the nooks and crevices on the wave-splashed rocks for amphipods, isopods and other small invertebrates that live hidden along the tide line.

Black Turnstones do much of their foraging by probing, but they have gained fame for an unusual feeding technique. As the name implies, the turnstone flips over small rocks and ocean debris with its bill to expose hidden invertebrates. The turnstone's bill is short, stubby and slightly up-turned—ideal for this foraging style.

Similar Species: Surfbird has yellowish-green legs and a terminal black band on its white tail; Wandering Tattler teeters and bobs as it feeds, it is light gray, and it is larger; Ruddy Turnstone has rust color in its wings and back.

Jan Feb Mar Apr May Jun Jul Aug Sept Oct Nov Dec

Quick I.D.: robin-sized; white belly; dark reddish-brown legs; stout, slightly upturned bill; sexes similar.
Breeding: black upperparts; white eyebrow and lore spot.
Non-breeding: dark brownish-gray upperparts.
Size: 9 in.

Greater Yellowlegs
Tringa melanoleuca

On a spring walk along the shores of San Leandro Bay, you may see a few sandpipers. The Greater Yellowlegs prefers shallow pools where it can peck for small invertebrates, but it may venture belly-deep into the water to pursue prey. Occasionally, a yellowlegs can be seen hopping along on one leg, with the other one tucked up in the body feathers to reduce heat loss.

Many birders enjoy the challenge of distinguishing the Greater Yellowlegs from the Lesser Yellowlegs. The Greater, which is more common on the West Coast (but don't let that bias your identification), has a relatively longer, heavier bill. The bill is also slightly upturned—so slightly that you notice it one moment and not the next. Generally, the Lesser calls with two *tews*, and the Greater calls with three. Cocky birders will name them at a glance, but more experienced birders will tell you that many of these people are bluffing, and that much of the time you can only write 'unidentified yellowlegs' in your field notes.

Similar Species: Lesser Yellowlegs is smaller and has a shorter bill; Western Sandpiper (p. 59), Sanderling (p. 60) and Dunlin (p. 61) are all much smaller and have dark legs.

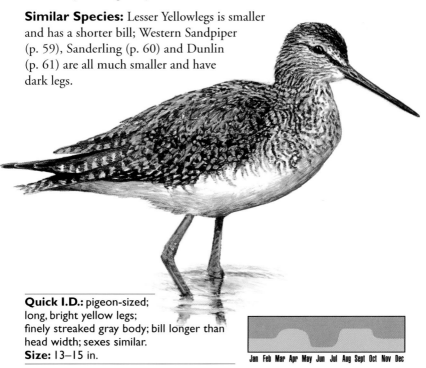

Quick I.D.: pigeon-sized; long, bright yellow legs; finely streaked gray body; bill longer than head width; sexes similar.
Size: 13–15 in.

Jan Feb Mar Apr May Jun Jul Aug Sept Oct Nov Dec

Spotted Sandpiper
Actitis macularia

This common shorebird of coasts, lakes and rivers has a most uncommon mating strategy. In a reversal of the gender roles of most birds, female Spotted Sandpipers compete for males in the spring. After the nest is built and the eggs are laid, the female leaves to find another mate, while the first male incubates the eggs. This behavior is repeated two or more times before the female settles down with one male to raise her last brood of chicks. Spotted Sandpipers occasionally nest in the San Francisco area, but they are most frequently encountered during the winter months along the undisturbed shores of large waterbodies.

The Spotted Sandpiper is readily identified by its arthritic-looking, stiff-winged flight low over water. Their peppy call—*eat-wheat wheat-wheat-wheat*—bursts from startled birds as they retreat from shoreline disturbances. Spotted Sandpipers constantly teeter and bob when not in flight, which makes them easy to identify.

Similar Species: Killdeer (p. 54) has dark throat bands; Greater Yellowlegs (p. 57) and Lesser Yellowlegs have longer legs; Dunlin (p. 61) has dark legs and is usually seen in large flocks; Wandering Tattler has no white in its wings.

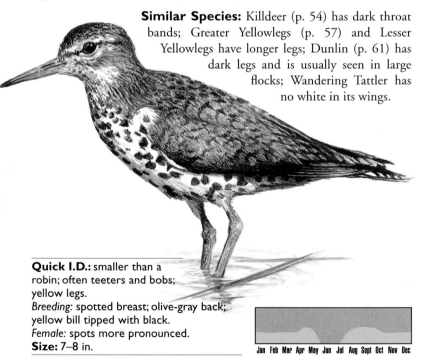

Quick I.D.: smaller than a robin; often teeters and bobs; yellow legs.
Breeding: spotted breast; olive-gray back; yellow bill tipped with black.
Female: spots more pronounced.
Size: 7–8 in.

Jan Feb Mar Apr May Jun Jul Aug Sept Oct Nov Dec

Western Sandpiper
Calidris mauri

Wintering Western Sandpipers look nondescript, but what they lack in defining plumage they make up in numbers and synchrony. At migration times in the fall and spring, thousands of these shorebirds huddle and forage along open mudflats, picking at the tiny organisms that live in the damp shorelines.

The challenge of identifying wintering shorebirds awaits the interested birder at Alameda South Shore. From July through September, many species of these confusing 'peeps' (as they are collectively called by birders) can be observed with patience, and at very close range. Even if the subtlety of plumage is not your primary interest, a morning spent with shuffling sandpipers will prove to be enjoyable.

Similar Species: Sanderling (p. 60) is larger and frequently runs in the surf; Dunlin (p. 61) is larger and has more brown on its head; Least Sandpiper is smaller and has pale legs.

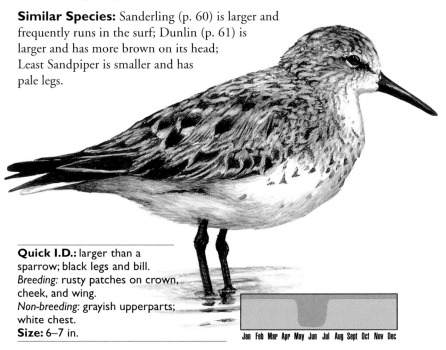

Quick I.D.: larger than a sparrow; black legs and bill. *Breeding:* rusty patches on crown, cheek, and wing. *Non-breeding:* grayish upperparts; white chest.
Size: 6–7 in.

Jan Feb Mar Apr May Jun Jul Aug Sept Oct Nov Dec

Sanderling
Calidris alba

A winter stroll along a sandy saltwater beach is occasionally punctuated by the sight of these tiny runners. They appear to enjoy nothing more than playing in the surf. Sanderlings are characteristically seen chasing and retreating from the rolling waves, never getting caught in the surf. Only the Sanderling commonly forages in this manner, plucking at the exposed invertebrates stirred up by the wave action. Without waves to chase along calm shorelines, Sanderlings daintily probe into wet soil in much the same fashion as many other sandpipers.

This sandpiper is one of the world's most widespread birds. It breeds across the Arctic in Alaska, Canada and Russia, and it spends the winter running up and down sandy shorelines in North America, South America, Asia, Africa and Australia.

Similar Species: Western Sandpiper (p. 59) and Least Sandpiper are smaller and darker; Dunlin (p. 61) is darker and has a downcurved bill.

Jan Feb Mar Apr May Jun Jul Aug Sept Oct Nov Dec

Quick I.D.: smaller than a robin; straight, black bill; dark legs.
Breeding (May): rusty head and breast.
Non-breeding: white underparts; grayish-white upperparts.
Size: 7¹/₂–8¹/₂ in.

Dunlin
Calidris alpina

The small, plump Dunlin is perhaps the most widespread winter shorebird in the San Francisco area. Flocks of these birds can occasionally be seen on both fresh- and saltwater shorelines. Although the flocks move about continuously around San Francisco Bay shorelines, Alameda South Shore and San Leandro Bay often host thousands of Dunlin through the winter. These tight flocks are generally more exclusive than many other shorebird troupes: few species mix with groups of Dunlin.

The Dunlin, like most other shorebirds, nests on the Arctic tundra and winters on the coasts of North America, Europe and Asia. It was originally called a 'Dunling' (meaning 'a small brown bird'), but for reasons lost to science the 'g' was later dropped.

Similar Species: Western Sandpiper (p. 59) and Least Sandpiper are smaller; Sanderling (p. 60) is paler and is usually seen running in the surf.

Quick I.D.: smaller than a robin; slightly downcurved bill; dark legs.
Breeding (April-May): black belly; streaked underparts; rusty back.
Non-breeding: pale gray underparts; grayish-brown upperparts.
Size: 9 in.

Jan Feb Mar Apr May Jun Jul Aug Sept Oct Nov Dec

Long-billed Curlew
Numenius americanus

If you visit a tidal mudflat from late July to April, you will see flocks of shorebirds foraging for soft-bodied invertebrates, small crabs and clams in the rich, soft substrate. After carefully watching these birds, you will begin to understand why so many different species can coexist in such high numbers. The secret lies in the different shapes and sizes of their bills. Most shorebirds forage in different manners—some pick up food at the surface, while others probe at various depths—which reduces competition over food between species.

The Long-billed Curlew's large size and sickle-shaped bill set this bird apart from its peers. Armed with a bill up to 7 inches long, this is one of the deepest probers on the tidal flats. Although good numbers can be seen seasonally at Bolinas Lagoon and at other shallow wetlands, the over-all population of curlews is declining because of the destruction of its grassland breeding grounds.

Similar Species: Marbled Godwit (p. 63) has a straight, two-toned bill; Whimbrel is smaller, has stripes on its crown and face, and lacks the cinnamon underwings.

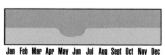

Jan Feb Mar Apr May Jun Jul Aug Sept Oct Nov Dec

Quick I.D.: duck-sized; long, downcurved bill; cinnamon-brown upperparts; cinnamon underwings; no prominent striping; sexes similar (except male has a shorter bill). **Size:** 20–25 in.

Marbled Godwit
Limosa fedoa

The lance-like bill of the Marbled Godwit may look plenty long enough to reach buried worms, amphipods and small clams, but the godwit doesn't seem content with its reach. It is frequently seen foraging with its head submerged beneath the water's surface, or with its face pressed against the mud. The deep probes appear to satisfy this large shorebird: godwits look genuinely pleased with a face full of mud!

The Marbled Godwit's bill is two-toned—light near the face and dark at the tip. The dark tip may give the bill extra strength, because black pigments are stronger than light-colored pigments.

Similar Species: Long-billed Curlew (p. 62) and Whimbrel have down-curved bills; Willet (p. 64) has black and white wings and a shorter bill; Short-billed Dowitcher (p. 65) and Long-billed Dowitcher have straight, dark bills.

Quick I.D.: smaller than a duck; long, slightly upturned, two-toned bill (dark at tip, pink at base); dark, mottled brown back; light brown underparts; sexes similar.
Size: 18 in.

Jan Feb Mar Apr May Jun Jul Aug Sept Oct Nov Dec

Willet
Catoptrophorus semipalmatus

These large, gray-brown sandpipers can be seen on tidal flats, along sandy shorelines (at Ocean and Thornton beaches) and in most wetlands. Foraging Willets can be confusing to beginning birdwatchers because resting birds have few diagnostic field marks and their winter plumage is dull. When Willets take wing, however, their flight feathers and wing linings are an unmistakable clash of black and white as they move from one foraging site to another. The call of this common shorebird is easily recognized. It sounds like a musical *will-will-willet will-willet*.

Similar Species: Greater Yellowlegs (p. 57) and Lesser Yellowlegs have yellow legs and a fine bill; Short-billed Dowitcher (p. 65) and Long-billed Dowitcher, Marbled Godwit (p. 63) and Whimbrel all lack the black-and-white wing patterning.

Jan Feb Mar Apr May Jun Jul Aug Sept Oct Nov Dec

Quick I.D.: larger than a pigeon; plump; gray; sexes similar.
Non-breeding: black-and-white wing patterning; dark, heavy bill; gray legs.
Size: 14–16 in.

Short-billed Dowitcher
Limnodromus griseus

When the winter tides are at their highest, shorebirds concentrate in large numbers along mudflats and estuaries in the Bay Area. High tides force dowitchers and other wintering shorebirds to high, dry ground, often packing them together in large numbers. Dowitchers tend to be stockier than most shorebirds, and they avoid deeper water. The sewing machine–like rhythms that dowitchers perform while foraging deeply into the mudflats is helpful for field identification.

Unfortunately, separating the two Bay Area dowitcher species is one of the most difficult tasks any birder may attempt. Although most people are perfectly content to simply call them Dowitchers, some birders insist they can separate the two species, which are extremely similar in winter plumage, by their voice.

Similar Species: Long-billed Dowitcher has barring on its sides and an unmarked breast, its plumage is darker over-all, and its bill is slightly longer; Common Snipe has longer legs, heavily barred upperparts and different foraging techniques.

Quick I.D.: larger than a robin; very long, straight, dark bill; very stocky body; short neck; sexes similar.
Breeding: reddish underparts; lightly barred flanks; dark, mottled upperparts; dark eyeline; light eyebrow; dark yellow legs; white rump.
Non-breeding: gray over-all; white belly.
Size: 11–12¹/₂ in. (female larger).

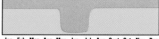

Jan Feb Mar Apr May Jun Jul Aug Sept Oct Nov Dec

American Avocet
Recurvirostra americana

Even in its subdued winter plumage, the American Avocet, with its graceful upturned bill and long, baby-blue legs, is one of the most elegant inhabitants of the Bay Area. In flight, its long legs and bill help make this slim bird look like a winged stick.

One of the common ways the American Avocet forages is by sweeping its bill quickly from side to side, just below the water's surface. Despite the whip-like quickness of this action, it is surprisingly effective at collecting tiny invertebrates suspended in the water. The American Avocet also uses a duck-like, tipped-up feeding behavior while swimming. It uses its partially webbed feet to negotiate areas of deep water.

Similar Species: Willet (p. 64) lacks the long bill and the long, trailing legs in flight; Black-necked Stilt (p. 67) lacks the upturned bill, and it has black extending from its crown to its back.

Quick I.D.: small gull–sized; long, upturned bill; black-and-white wings; light underparts; gray-blue legs; sexes similar (except female has a more curved bill).
Winter: light gray head and breast.
Size: 17–18 in.

Jan Feb Mar Apr May Jun Jul Aug Sept Oct Nov Dec

Black-necked Stilt
Himantopus mexicanus

Quick I.D.: larger than a pigeon; very long, pinkish (red) legs; dark upperparts; clean white underparts; long, straight, needle-like, black bill; small white eyebrow; sexes similar (but male has slightly blacker upperparts).
Size: 13¹/₂–15¹/₂ in.

Jan Feb Mar Apr May Jun Jul Aug Sept Oct Nov Dec

On long, gangly legs, the Black-necked Stilt strides daintily through shallow pools, brackish ponds and Bay Area salt evaporators. Its grace, beauty and fragility are highlights in sometimes desolate and unassuming habitats. Purposeful in each stride, stilts walk and peck at the moist substrate and the water's surface with their long needle-like bill. These shorebirds eat a variety of waterbugs, waterbeetles, and small crustaceans, which they catch with pinpoint accuracy. Males tend to be slightly larger and longer-legged than females, and they forage in deeper water, which reduces the competition for food.

Similar Species: American Avocet (p. 66) lacks the black crown, and it has an up-curved bill and baby blue legs; Black Oystercatcher is all-black and has a red bill.

Western Gull
Larus occidentalis

This abundant resident of the southern Pacific coast is known to all Bay Area residents. These large, dark-backed gulls are easily encountered on a daily basis, and they are routinely seen soaring overhead or standing along a shoreline. The thousands of Western Gulls in the Bay Area help keep seashores, parking lots and city parks free of decaying animal matter.

Western Gulls are the only gulls to nest in the San Francisco area, and the Farallon Islands host between 22,000 and 25,000 pairs yearly. Thousands of other seabirds also nest on these islands, which in turn provides Western Gulls with a seasonal bounty of eggs and young. Although these gulls prey on the nests and young of many seabirds, the colonies of these other species still survive and flourish.

Similar Species: Glaucous-winged Gull (p. 70) has a light gray back and wing covers, black eyes and gray wingtips; Mew Gull (p. 71) is much smaller and has black eyes and an all-yellow bill; California Gull (p. 72) has yellow legs and is smaller; Herring Gull (winter resident) has a lighter back and wing covers; Heermann's Gull is darker and has a red bill.

Quick I.D.: large gull; dark gray back and wing covers; white head; black wingtips; pink legs; yellow bill; yellow eye; sexes similar.
Juvenile: mottled brown over-all.
Size: 24–26 in.

Jan Feb Mar Apr May Jun Jul Aug Sept Oct Nov Dec

Ring-billed Gull
Larus delawarensis

As August rolls through the San Francisco area, Ring-billed Gulls return from their nesting sites on the Great Basin to overwinter along the coast. These mid-sized gulls do not make up a majority of the gull flocks in San Francisco, but their bills are sufficiently distinctive to set them apart from the more numerous species in the area. The black ring around both the upper and lower mandible does not reach the bill's tip, which is as yellow as the rest of the bill.

During the winter, Ring-billed Gulls can be encountered throughout the San Francisco region. They associate with other flocks of gulls in city parks, in shopping center parking lots, in fast food restaurants and on lakes and ponds. They can often be seen along the shores of Lake Merritt in Oakland. Along beaches, Ring-billed Gulls eat dead fish, birds and other animal matter, while inland they take worms, garbage and waste grain.

Similar Species: Glaucous-winged Gull (p. 70) has a dark eye, lacks the bill ring, is much larger and has pink legs and gray wingtips; Mew Gull (p. 71) has a dark eye and lacks the bill ring; California Gull (p. 72) is larger, lacks the bill ring and has a dark eye; Herring Gull is larger, has pink legs and lacks the bill ring; Heermann's Gull is darker and has a red bill and an all-yellow bill.

Quick I.D.: mid-sized gull; black ring near bill tip; yellow bill and legs; dark gray wing covers; light eye; black wingtips; small white spots on black primaries; white underparts; sexes similar.
Non-breeding: white head and nape washed with brown.
First winter: mottled grayish brown; gray back; blackish-brown primaries; brown band on tail.
Size: 18–20 in.

Jan Feb Mar Apr May Jun Jul Aug Sept Oct Nov Dec

Glaucous-winged Gull

Larus glaucescens

The Glaucous-winged Gull is a winter resident in the San Francisco area. It has been able to adapt readily to the urbanization of the region, and it can truly be found anywhere and everywhere. Large flocks of this gull can be found in bays, estuaries, freshwater lakes, garbage dumps, city parks and agricultural fields. Glaucous-winged Gulls are so widely dispersed that they are sure to be sighted on just about any birding trip along the San Francisco Bay shoreline.

A very similar species, the Western Gull, commonly breeds in the San Francisco area. Many hybrids of the two species winter in the San Francisco area. These hybrids look very much like pure Glaucous-wings except that their wingtips are dusky.

A rewarding exercise for novice birdwatchers is to glance over a flock of 50 or so birds. Within a few minutes, even the most inexperienced birder will begin to sort out the gulls based on their size and on the color of their eyes, wingtips and legs.

Similar Species: Herring Gull has pink feet, yellow eyes and black wingtips; Western Gull (p. 68) has a dark back, dark wings, yellow eyes and black wingtips; Ring-billed Gull (p. 69) and California Gull (p. 72) have black wingtips and yellow-green feet.

Quick I.D.: large gull; white head and body; pale gray wingtips; light gray back and wings; pink legs; dark eyes; red spot on lower mandible; sexes similar. *Non-breeding* and *Immature:* variable.
Size: 24–27 in.

Jan Feb Mar Apr May Jun Jul Aug Sept Oct Nov Dec

Mew Gull
Larus canus

The Mew Gulls that overwinter along San Francisco Bay are not regular visitors to the local landfills. These small gulls, named after one of their calls, forego quick and convenient human leftovers for natural foods. Mew Gulls can be seen foraging in the lakes of Golden Gate Park, where they frequently land on the water to pick up floating matter. A Mew Gull will occasionally plunge its head beneath the water, but it seldom dives. Only during heavy winter rains are these gulls commonly seen on land, when they feed in large numbers on park lawns. These common winter visitors nest in northern British Columbia, Alaska and Siberia.

Like other marine birds, the Mew Gull has specialized glands around the eyes near the base of the bill that help it cope with the salt it ingests when drinking saltwater. The glands extract salt from the blood and produce a concentrated salty liquid that can be seen dripping from the birds' bills.

Similar Species: Western (p. 68), Ring-billed (p. 69), Glaucous-winged (p. 70), California (p. 72), Herring and Thayer's gulls are all much larger; Bonaparte's Gull has a black hood or ear patch and a white flash in the wings.

Quick I.D.: small gull; white head and body; light gray wings; black wingtips; yellow legs; dark eyes; sexes similar.
Size: 16–18 in.

Jan Feb Mar Apr May Jun Jul Aug Sept Oct Nov Dec

California Gull
Larus californicus

California Gulls leave their breeding grounds to trickle back to the coast starting in late June; most of them have arrived by August and will stay for the following eight months. They winter exclusively on the West Coast, from the Pacific Northwest down through Baja California.

When at their breeding grounds on the prairies, California Gulls feed on grasshoppers. They are celebrated in Salt Lake City, where a voracious flock of gulls saved the crops of settlers from an outbreak of ravenous grasshoppers in 1848.

Similar Species: Western Gull (p. 68) and Herring Gull are larger and have light eyes; Ring-billed Gull (p. 69) has light eyes and a ring around its bill; Glaucous-winged Gull (p. 70) is larger and has light gray wingtips; Mew Gull (p. 71) is much smaller; Thayer's Gull has dark pink feet; Heermann's Gull is uniformly slate-gray, and it has a red bill and black legs.

Jan Feb Mar Apr May Jun Jul Aug Sept Oct Nov Dec

Quick I.D.: mid-sized gull; white head and body; gray wings; black wingtips; greenish-yellow legs; dark eyes; sexes similar.
Size: 21 in.

Forster's Tern
Sterna forsteri

Quick I.D.: larger than a pigeon; orange legs and feet; white underparts; mostly gray tail; light gray wing covers; thin bill; sexes similar.
In flight: shallowly forked tail; white rump; long, pointed wings.
Breeding: black cap; orange bill tipped in black.
Non-breeding: grayish cap; black mask over eyes; black bill.
Size: 14–15 in.

Jan Feb Mar Apr May Jun Jul Aug Sept Oct Nov Dec

Wheeling about in mid-air to a stationary hover, the Forster's Tern carefully measures up its task; then it dives quickly into the water. The headfirst dive is often rewarded with the catch of a small fish, which is carried away in the bird's thin bill. The Forster's Tern breeds and winters in the Bay Area, and it can routinely be seen in foraging flights 10 to 20 yards above calm waters.

Terns fly effortlessly, bouncing lazily up and down in the rhythm of their wingbeats. They superficially resemble gulls in body form, but their behavior differs dramatically. Terns rarely soar in the air, and they are infrequently seen resting on the water. While flying, terns usually have their bills pointed towards the ground and their forked tails are usually visible.

Similar Species: Caspian Tern (p. 74) is much larger and has an all-red bill; Common Tern has a darker red bill and legs, a mostly white tail and dark-tipped primaries; Least Tern (rare) is much smaller and has a white forehead; Elegant Tern is larger and has a longer orange bill and a black crest.

Caspian Tern
Sterna caspia

Quick I.D.: gull-sized; black cap; heavy, blood-red bill; light gray wing covers; white underparts; black legs; sexes similar.
In flight: shallowly forked tail; long, pointed wings; head pointed downwards.
Size: 19–22¹/₂ in.

Jan Feb Mar Apr May Jun Jul Aug Sept Oct Nov Dec

Perhaps no other bird possesses such an odd North American breeding distribution as the Caspian Tern. Isolated colonies of Caspian Terns breed in pockets in Utah, in Wyoming, in British Columbia, in the Northwest Territories, near the Great Lakes, in Newfoundland and on the Pacific Coast of the United States. In the San Francisco Bay Area, the Caspian Tern nests in disturbed or human-created habitats, such as dikes and shorelines.

The Caspian Tern is the largest tern in North America, and it can be confused in flight only with gulls. Although it is the size of some of the area's smaller gulls, the Caspian Tern is easily identified by its lazy, stiff flight and its coral red bill. The species never reaches the abundance of many other gulls and terns in the Bay Area, but its formidable size results in a second look each spring from birders who have grown accustomed throughout the winter to the smaller Forster's Tern.

Similar Species: Forster's Tern (p. 73) and Common Tern are both much smaller and lack the heavy, red bill; Elegant Tern has a thin orange bill and a black crest; Western Gull (p. 68) lacks the red bill and the black cap.

Common Murre
Uria aalge

Like all alcids, Common Murres appear more comfortable on the sea than in the air. Their tiny wings are designed for pursuing fish underwater, and in flight they beat the air feverishly as they attempt to maintain speed. Like uncontrolled missiles, murres veer from side to side as they rocket over the ocean. During the fall and winter, Common Murres can be seen flying offshore past the Cliff House, and occasionally they can be closely observed as they drift with the current not far from shore. In late summer, adults and young can be seen from ferry boats in San Francisco Bay.

Many birds that live on saltwater share the countershading coloration of the murre. From above, the dark back blends with the steely sea, while submerged predators and prey cannot find the light-colored underbelly against the bright sky. Unfortunately, gill nets lying hidden below the ocean surface claim many of these large alcids each year.

Similar Species: All other alcids and sea ducks lack the combination of a long, slender bill and distinctive countershading; Common Loon (p. 18) is much larger and has a bigger head; Horned Grebe (p. 20) is smaller and has a longer neck; Western Grebe (p. 21) has a long, slim neck.

Quick I.D.: crow-sized; black upperparts; white underparts; sexes similar.
Breeding: black head and neck.
Non-breeding: white neck and chin.
Size: 16–17 in.

Jan Feb Mar Apr May Jun Jul Aug Sept Oct Nov Dec

Pigeon Guillemot
Cepphus columba

Quick I.D.: pigeon-sized; bright red feet and mouth; white wing patch; long neck; sexes similar.
Breeding: black over-all.
Non-breeding: light head and underparts; dark back.
Size: 12–14 in.

Jan Feb Mar Apr May Jun Jul Aug Sept Oct Nov Dec

Pigeon Guillemots are common seabirds that forage near shore and nest on rocky cliff ledges. The solid black breeding plumage surrounding a white wing patch is offset by the guillemot's radiant red mouth-lining and feet. These scarlet accents are flaunted outrageously during courtship rituals, when guillemots wave their feet and then peer down the throats of potential mates. The bold markings enable birdwatchers to easily spot Pigeon Guillemots nesting on brown cliffs. Guillemots have nested on the bluffs of Lincoln Park and Point Bonita.

Similar Species: Ancient Murrelet and Marbled Murrelet are smaller and lack the white wing patch; Rhinoceros Auklet has a more robust body form and a thicker bill, and it lacks the white wing patch.

Rock Dove
Columba livia

The Rock Dove (or pigeon) is very dependent on humans for food and shelter. This Eurasian native lives in old buildings, on ledges and on bridges, and it feeds primarily on waste grain and human handouts.

Rock Doves may appear strained when walking—their heads moving back and forth with every step—but few birds are as agile in flight, or as abundant in urban and industrial areas. While no other bird varies as much in coloration, all Rock Doves, whether white, red, blue or mixed-pigment, will clap their wings above and below their bodies upon take-off.

Similar Species: Band-tailed Pigeon (p. 78) is larger, has a grayish tail band and lacks the white rump; Mourning Dove (p. 79) is the same length as the Rock Dove, but it is slender and has a long, tapering tail and olive-brown plumage.

Quick I.D.: mid-sized pigeon; variable color (iridescent blue-gray, black, red or white); white rump (usually); orange feet; fleshy base to bill; sexes similar.
Size: 13–14 in.

Jan Feb Mar Apr May Jun Jul Aug Sept Oct Nov Dec

Band-tailed Pigeon
Columba fasciata

Band-tailed Pigeons can be seen flying over our wooded hillsides every day of the year, but few people take note of them since they appear so similar to Rock Doves. Band-tails are our native pigeon, and these secretive birds appear bulkier in flight than their ubiquitous and introduced counterpart. During the breeding season, individual birds are seen as 'flybys,' and they flock together only while feeding or roosting in trees.

Band-tailed Pigeons are awkward feeders, as can be observed in many of our forested city parks and golf courses. The birds cling clumsily to branches that bend under their weight. As the pigeons yo-yo up and down, they carefully pluck at the fruits of the Pacific madrone, which they find particularly appealing. Band-tails also visit backyard feeders in the early morning hours, usually cleaning them out before the homeowner awakes. Band-tailed Pigeons build their well-concealed nests among the upper branches of Douglas-fir or redwood trees.

Similar Species: Rock Dove (p. 77) is slightly smaller, has orange legs and usually has a white rump and white underwings.

Quick I.D.: large pigeon; purple head and chest; white band at back of neck; grayish band on tail; gray rump; yellow bill tipped with black; dark underwings; sexes similar.
Size: 14–15¹/₂.

Jan Feb Mar Apr May Jun Jul Aug Sept Oct Nov Dec

Mourning Dove
Zenaida macroura

As a Mourning Dove bursts into flight, its wings 'clap' above and below its body for the first few wingbeats. The Mourning Dove is a swift, direct flier, and its wings can be heard whistling through the air. When not in flight, the peaceful *cooooo-cooooo-cooooah* call of the Mourning Dove can be heard filtering through open woodlands. These year-round residents roost inconspicuously in trees, but their soft cooing often betrays their presence.

The Mourning Dove feeds primarily on the ground, picking up grain and grit in open areas. It builds a flat, loose stick nest that rests flimsily on branches and trunks. Mourning Doves are attentive parents and, like other members of the pigeon family, they feed 'milk' to their young. It isn't true milk—since birds lack mammary glands— but a fluid produced by glands in the bird's crop. The chicks insert their bills down the adult's throat to eat the thick liquid.

Similar Species: Rock Dove (p. 77) has a white rump, is stockier and has a shorter tail; Band-tailed Pigeon (p. 78) has a shorter tail, and its plumage tends to be darker gray.

Quick I.D: larger than a jay; gray-brown plumage; long, white-trimmed, tapering tail; sleek body; dark, shinny patch below ear; orange feet; dark bill; peach-colored underparts; sexes similar.
Size: 11–13 in.

Jan Feb Mar Apr May Jun Jul Aug Sept Oct Nov Dec

Barn Owl
Tyto alba

Barn Owls and humans have gradually entered into a mutually beneficial relationship. Before European colonization, Barn Owls nested primarily in snags, hollow trees and caves, hunting voles and mice in shrublands. With the arrival of Europeans and their rodent associates (house mice and black rats), however, the Barn Owl's diet underwent a slight shift. Barn Owls now commonly roost in old buildings and barns as well as in natural cavities, and they primarily hunt non-native rodents, much to the delight of present-day residents, who view the rodents as agricultural and esthetic pests. Barn Owls have not been a complete benefactor of urbanization, however, and some die each year in vehicular accidents and from human usage of pesticides.

Similar Species: Great Horned Owl (p. 82) is darker gray and has ear tufts and yellow eyes.

Quick I.D.: crow-sized; white, heart-shaped face; dark eyes; light underparts; golden-brown upperparts; sexes similar.
Size: 16 in.

Jan Feb Mar Apr May Jun Jul Aug Sept Oct Nov Dec

Western Screech-Owl
Otus kennicottii

Despite its small size, the Western Screech-Owl is an adaptable hunter. It has a varied diet that ranges from insects, earthworms and fish to birds larger than itself. Silent and reclusive by day, screech-owls hunt at night.

Some owls' senses are refined for darkness and their bodies for silence. Their large, forward-facing eyes have many times more light-gathering sensors than do ours, and the wings of nocturnal owls are edged with frayed feathers for silent flight. Their ears, located on the sides of their heads, are asymmetrical (one is higher than the other), which enables these birds to track sounds more easily.

Given these adaptations, it is no surprise that owls have successfully invaded nearly all of the world's major ecosystems. Strolling along the wooded paths of our larger wooded parks (such as Tilden and Redwood regional parks) during early spring evenings, a person with a keen ear will hear the distinctive whistled voice of the Western Screech-Owl. The call's rhythm has often been compared to that of a bouncing ball coming to rest.

Similar Species: Northern Saw-whet Owl has a dark facial disc and no ear tufts, and its call does not increase in pace.

Quick I.D.: robin-sized; short ear tufts; heavy vertical streaking on chest; yellow eyes; dark bill; sexes similar.
Size: 8–9 in. (female slightly larger).

Jan Feb Mar Apr May Jun Jul Aug Sept Oct Nov Dec

Great Horned Owl
Bubo virginianus

The Great Horned Owl is the most widely distributed owl in North America, and it is among the most formidable of coastal predators. It uses specialized hearing, powerful talons and human-sized eyes during nocturnal hunts for mice, rabbits, quail, amphibians and occasionally fish. It has a poorly developed sense of smell, which is why it can prey on skunks. Worn-out and discarded Great Horned Owl feathers are therefore often identifiable by a simple sniff.

The deep, resonant hooting of the Great Horned Owl is easily imitated, often leading to interesting exchanges between bird and birder. The call's deep tone is not as distinctive as its pace, which closely follows the rhythm of *eat my food, I'll-eat yooou*.

Similar Species: Spotted Owl has no ear tufts; Western Screech-Owl (p. 81) is much smaller and has vertical breast streaking; Long-eared Owl has a slimmer body and vertical streaks on its chest, and its ear tufts are very close together.

Jan Feb Mar Apr May Jun Jul Aug Sept Oct Nov Dec

Quick I.D.: hawk-sized; large, widely spaced ear tufts; fine, horizontal chest bars; dark brown plumage; white throat; sexes similar.
Size: 18–25 in.

Anna's Hummingbird
Calypte anna

The male Anna's Hummingbird is the most distinctive hummingbird in the Bay Area. Although residents meet many hummingbirds in their gardens and city parks, no other male 'hummer' has its head and neck draped in a similar rose-red splendor that dances with the sun's rays: Anna's is the only hummingbird on the continent to show this feature.

The Anna's Hummingbird nests in backyard gardens, chaparral shrublands, oak woodlands and savannahs. Following its early spring nesting period, most birds undergo a post-breeding movement to the north and upslope to take advantage of late-blooming flowers. Once the cool winds of late summer begin to blow through the high country, most Anna's Hummingbirds in the Bay Area retreat to the lowlands for the remainder of the year.

Similar Species: Male is distinctive; females of Allen's Hummingbird (p. 84) and Rufous Hummingbird have rufous-brown flanks.

Quick I.D.: iridescent green upperparts; white underparts; long, narrow bill.
Male: rose throat and head; green band around waist.
Female: green crown; rose-spotted throat; light green flanks.
Size: 3¹/₂–4¹/₂ in.

Jan Feb Mar Apr May Jun Jul Aug Sept Oct Nov Dec

Allen's Hummingbird
Selasphorus sasin

Quick I.D.: much smaller than a sparrow; iridescent green head and back; long dark bill; red flanks.
Male: bright red throat; white breast; rufous vest.
Female: red-spotted throat; white underparts.
Size: 3–4 in.

Jan Feb Mar Apr May Jun Jul Aug Sept Oct Nov Dec

The Allen's Hummingbird arrives in the Bay Area in late January, timing its appearance to coincide with the flowering of native and garden shrubs. Males quickly establish territories among the coastal scrub, chaparral, eucalyptus and cypress groves, as well as in parks and gardens. These small, pugnacious tyrants perch high atop shrubs and trees, surveying their territories from a commanding platform. Should any rival dare to cross the bird's boundary, it is quickly met with a noisy and aggressive welcome. The tiny birds whirr about at great speeds and often disappear past surrounding shrubs still tailing the intruder.

The drab females incubate the eggs alone, in a nest no greater in diameter than a silver dollar. Unless they are built in a backyard garden, the tiny, well-concealed hummingbird nests are seldom seen.

Similar Species: Male Anna's Hummingbird (p. 83) has a rose throat and head; female Anna's Hummingbird has gray flanks and a rose-spotted throat; male Rufous Hummingbird (mainly a migrant) has a rufous back; female Rufous Hummingbird is indistinguishable from female Allen's.

Belted Kingfisher
Ceryle alcyon

The Belted Kingfisher is found year-round near quiet waters, never far from shore. As the name suggests, kingfishers primarily prey on fish, which they catch with precise headfirst dives. A dead branch extending over fresh- or saltwater will often serve as a perch from which to survey the fish below.

The Belted Kingfisher builds its nest near the end of a long tunnel excavated a few feet into sandy or dirt banks. A rattling call, blue-gray coloration and a large crest are the distinctive features of the Belted Kingfisher. With most birds the males are more colorful, but female Kingfishers are distinguished from males by the presence of a second, rust-colored band across the upper chest.

Although there are many species of kingfisher in the world, the Belted Kingfisher is the only member of its family across most of the United States. The San Francisco area is blessed with year-round open water, and Belted Kingfishers can be encountered every day of the year, crashing into calm waters in search of fish.

Similar Species: None.

Quick I.D.: pigeon-sized; blue-gray back, wings and head; shaggy crest; heavy bill. *Male:* single, blue chest band. *Female:* blue chest band; rust-colored belt.
Size: 12–14 in.

Jan Feb Mar Apr May Jun Jul Aug Sept Oct Nov Dec

Acorn Woodpecker
Melanerpes formicivorus

In almost every sizable oak woodlot in our region lives a bird with habits that excite behavioral ecologists. The Acorn Woodpecker occurs over a relatively small geographic range, but its foraging and reproductive habits have given it worldwide recognition. These highly social woodpeckers remain in family units of up to a dozen related birds. Only a pair or two may actually breed, and the remainder of the group helps the parents raise the young.

Communal breeding is very uncommon in birds, and it may be explained in the Acorn Woodpecker's case by its unusual food-hoarding behavior. The Acorn Woodpecker eats a wide variety of food items, from fruit to insects—the species name means 'ant eater'—and family groups store huge quantities of acorns (up to 20,000) in decaying trees. The family uses its acorn larder as an insurance policy against food shortages during the winter. The larders require so much energy to collect and defend that it is possible only a sizable family group can effectively maintain one.

Similar Species: Other woodpeckers lack the solid black back, white forehead and red cap.

Quick I.D.: smaller than a robin; black wings with white patches; white rump; black tail; white cheeks and forehead; black chin.
Male: large red crown.
Female: small red crown on back of head.
Size: 9 in.

Jan Feb Mar Apr May Jun Jul Aug Sept Oct Nov Dec

Downy Woodpecker
Picoides pubescens

The Downy Woodpecker is a systematic forager, methodically chipping off dead bark and probing into crevices in search of hidden insects. Because of its small bill, the Downy Woodpecker can find food where larger-billed woodpeckers cannot reach. The black-and-white Downy Woodpecker is the smallest North American woodpecker, and it is common in wooded ravines and most wooded city parks. It is easily attracted to backyard feeders that offer suet.

As with other woodpeckers, the structure of the Downy Woodpecker's feet and tail help it climb vertically. It can clamp onto a trunk with its two forward-facing and two backward-facing toes, and it can prop its stiff tail against the trunk to steady itself.

Similar Species: Hairy Woodpecker is larger, and it has a longer bill and clean white outer tail feathers.

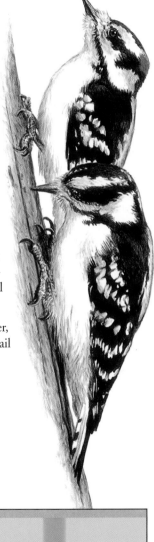

Quick I.D.: large sparrow–sized; black-and-white wings and back; unmarked, white underparts; short, stubby bill; white outer tail feather is spotted black.
Male: red patch on back of head.
Female: no red patch.
Size: 6–7 in.

Jan Feb Mar Apr May Jun Jul Aug Sept Oct Nov Dec

Nuttall's Woodpecker
Picoides nuttallii

The Nuttall's Woodpecker can often be seen hopping acrobatically on the undersides of branches and scaling up and down trunks. This woodpecker is fairly common in open deciduous forests, especially oak woodlands. It seems to prefer mature oak forests, but individuals are occasionally encountered in eucalyptus and cypress woodlands in the interior or on the coast.

This energetic woodpecker was named for one of America's early naturalists, Thomas Nuttall. Nuttall was primarily a botanist, but he traveled widely across the country, observing all aspects of natural history. Nuttall's many contributions to ornithology include his *Manual of Ornithology of the United States and Canada,* the first field guide ever written about North American birds.

Similar Species: Acorn Woodpecker (p. 86) has an all-black back; Downy Woodpecker (p. 87) and Hairy Woodpecker lack barring on their backs.

Jan Feb Mar Apr May Jun Jul Aug Sept Oct Nov Dec

Quick I.D.: larger than a sparrow; black-and-white barring on back; black cheek; dark spots on flanks.
Male: red cap on back of head.
Female: no red cap.
Size: 7¹/₂ in.

Northern Flicker
Colaptes auratus

Quick I.D.: jay-sized; brown-barred back; spotted underparts; black bib; white rump; long bill.
Red-shafted (main form in California): red wing and tail linings; brown crown.
Yellow-shafted (rare in California in winter): yellow wing and tail linings; gray crown; red nape.
Male red-shafted: red mustache.
Male yellow-shafted: black mustache
Female: no mustache.
Size: 11–14 in.

Jan Feb Mar Apr May Jun Jul Aug Sept Oct Nov Dec

Walkers strolling through Golden Gate Park may be surprised by a woodpecker flushing from the ground before them. As the Northern Flicker beats a hasty retreat, it reveals an unmistakable white rump and red wing linings. It is the least arboreal of our woodpeckers, and it spends more time feeding on the ground than other woodpeckers. Often, it is only when the Northern Flicker is around its nest cavity in a tree that it truly behaves like other woodpeckers: clinging, rattling and drumming.

The Northern Flicker can easily be seen all year, and it occasionally visits backyard feeders. The Northern Flicker (and other birds) squash ants and then preen themselves with the remains. Ants contain concentrations of formic acid, which is believed to kills small parasites living on the flicker's skin and in its feathers.

Similar Species: Other woodpeckers, Varied Thrush and American Robin (p. 113) all lack the white rump and red wing linings.

Olive-sided Flycatcher
Contopus borealis

A large bee weaving through the crowns of a conifer grove attracts the attention of an Olive-sided Flycatcher perched on a toppled tree. The bird launches and, after a few quick flaps of its wings, seizes the bee in mid-air. Holding its catch firmly in its bill, the bird loops back and lands on the same perch it vacated moments earlier. This is the art of flycatching, and the Olive-sided Flycatcher is a master of this acrobatic feeding technique.

No errant insect appears safe if it flies into the range of the Olive-sided Flycatcher, and no woodland grove is free from this bird's distinctive call. Offered from the highest perch, the Olive-sided Flycatcher's characteristic *quick three beers* is one of the easiest calls to identify.

Similar Species: Other flycatchers and Western Wood-Pewee all lack the dark, open vest.

Quick I.D.: smaller than a robin; dark olive vest with tufts of 'white shirt hanging out'; white throat and belly; dark tail and flight feathers; olive head and back; sexes similar.
Size: 7–8 in.

Jan Feb Mar Apr May Jun Jul Aug Sept Oct Nov Dec

Pacific-slope Flycatcher
Empidonax difficilis

Fortunately for birders, the Pacific-slope Flycatcher's song is much more distinctive than its plumage. When you enter any moist woodland during the spring, the Flycatcher's snappy *pawee* is always one of the first sounds you'll hear. This common songbird, formerly grouped with the Cordilleran Flycatcher into a single species—the Western Flycatcher—arrives in San Francisco in March and leaves before the end of September.

The genus name *Empidonax* means, quite appropriately, 'lord of the mosquitoes,' and this bird uses the foraging technique made famous by its family. From its perch on a shady limb, this small bird launches after a flying insect, seizes it in mid-air and loops back to alight on the same perch it vacated.

Similar Species: Willow Flycatcher (uncommon migrant) has a very faint eye-ring, and its song is *fitz-bew*; Western Wood-Pewee has no eye-ring and is dusky-colored; Olive-sided Flycatcher (p. 90) has a dark vest, and its song is *quick-three-beers*.

Quick I.D.: sparrow-sized; olive-green upperparts; yellow-green underparts; white eye-ring; two wing bars; dark bill; yellow wash on belly; dark wings and tail; sexes similar.
Size: 5–6 in.

Jan Feb Mar Apr May Jun Jul Aug Sept Oct Nov Dec

Black Phoebe
Sayornis nigricans

Quick I.D.: sparrow-sized; black upperparts, tail and chest; white belly and undertail coverts; sexes similar.
Size: 6¹/₂–7¹/₂ in.

Jan Feb Mar Apr May Jun Jul Aug Sept Oct Nov Dec

Unlike many flycatchers, the Black Phoebe often flycatches from a low perch and then alights on a different perch after seizing an insect. It usually builds a mud and grass nest under a bridge, culvert, picnic shelter or eave to gain refuge from the California rains. Because the Black Phoebe constructs its small cup nest one mouthful at a time, it often selects a site near a mud puddle to save on valuable construction time. Some Black Phoebes are present year-round, while others are migratory. Many can be watched wagging their tails from a fencetop perch in your backyard.

Similar Species: Other flycatchers tend to be olive-green or brown; Dark-eyed Junco (p. 132) has a rusty back and flanks and a conical bill, and it feeds mainly on the ground.

White-throated Swift
Aeronautes saxatalis

The White-throated Swift is one of the frequent fliers of the bird world; only incubation keeps this bird off its wings. It feeds, drinks, bathes and even mates in flight. During its 10- to 11-year average lifespan, these sailors of the air may travel more than 1 million miles.

The White-throated Swift is a year-round resident of the Bay Area, and it can be encountered on a daily basis throughout the summer. These high-flying aeronauts often forage for flying insects at great heights, and they are often visible only as sky specks. This swift nests on vertical crevices, which in the Bay Area includes cliffs, horizontal cracks, headlands, buildings and overpasses.

Similar Species: Vaux's Swift and Black Swift lack the contrasting white and dark underparts; Northern Rough-winged Swallow (p. 96) and Bank Swallow lack the dark flanks and the wing 'pits.'

Quick I.D.: black upperparts; white throat tapering to belly; black flanks; slender, sleek body; very small legs; sexes similar.
In flight: long, tapering wings that angle back; long, shallowly forked tail.
Size: 6¹/₂–7 in.

Jan Feb Mar Apr May Jun Jul Aug Sept Oct Nov Dec

SWIFTS AND SWALLOWS 93

Tree Swallow
Tachycineta bicolor

Depending on food availability, Tree Swallows may forage over great distances, darting above open fields and wetlands as they catch flying insects in their bills. These bicolored birds occasionally sweep down to the water surface for a quick drink and bath. In bad weather, Tree Swallows may fly up to 5 miles to distant marshes or lakes to find flying insects.

The Tree Swallow is among the first migrants to arrive in the San Francisco area, often beating the onset of spring weather. It returns to Lake Merced, Rodeo Lagoon and other freshwater marshes in mid-February to begin its reproductive cycle. It nests in abandoned woodpecker cavities as well as in nest boxes. The cavity is lined with weeds, grasses and long feathers. When the parents leave the eggs for long periods of time, the swallows cover them with the feathers. The females lay and incubate four to six eggs for up to 16 days. Once the birds hatch, the young leave the cavity within three weeks to begin their aerial lives.

Similar Species: Northern Rough-winged Swallow (p. 96) and Bank Swallow lack the green upperparts; Violet-green Swallow has a white cheek and a white rump patch.

Quick I.D.: sparrow-sized; iridescent blue-green plumage; white underparts; no white on cheek; dark rump; small bill; long, pointed wings; shallowly forked tail; small feet; sexes similar.
Size: 5–6 in.

Jan Feb Mar Apr May Jun Jul Aug Sept Oct Nov Dec

Cliff Swallow
Hirundo pyrrhonota

The Cliff Swallow is the most widespread swallow in San Francisco, and you can often encounter it in the hundreds. Cliff Swallows nest under many of the bridges that span our waters, and clouds of them will sometimes whip up on either side of a bridge. They do not restrict their nesting to bridges, however, and colonies are occasionally found under piers and on vacated structures and dry, rocky cliffs.

If you stop to inspect the undersides of a bridge, you may see hundreds of gourd-shaped nests stuck to the pillars and structural beams. The nests are meticulously made from mud, one mouthful at a time. As they busily build their nests, hundreds of Cliff Swallows create a chaotic scene with their constant procession back and forth between nest and mudflat.

Similar Species: Tree Swallow (p. 94) has a blue-green back; Northern Rough-winged Swallow (p. 96) and Vaux's Swift lack the light rump and forehead and the rusty cheeks; Barn Swallow (p. 97) has a deeply forked tail and a dark rump.

Quick I.D.: sparrow-sized; pale forehead; buff rump; dark back with white stripes; gray-brown wings and tail; white underparts; rusty cheeks; dark bib; square tail; sexes similar.
Size: 5–6 in.

Jan Feb Mar Apr May Jun Jul Aug Sept Oct Nov Dec

Northern Rough-winged Swallow
Stelgidopteryx serripennis

Northern Rough-winged Swallows cruise over wetlands, fields and meadows at low altitudes, catching flying insects gracefully in flight. They often catch transforming insects just as they are emerging from the water to enter their adult stage.

Northern Rough-winged Swallows begin nesting in April. They often use the old burrows of kingfishers, other swallows or mammals, as well as other similar sites. They do not appear to dig their own burrows, and they have recently adapted to human structures such as buildings and culverts. Rough-wings are not as colonial as some other swallow species; they prefer to nest in isolated pairs or in small, loose colonies.

Similar Species: Tree Swallow (p. 94) has green or blue upperparts; Bank Swallow has a dark chest band; Violet-green Swallow has green upperparts, a white cheek and a white rump patch.

Quick I.D.: sparrow-sized; brown upperparts; light underparts; no band on chest; long, pointed wings; small bill; dark cheek; dark rump; small legs; sexes similar. **Size:** 5–6 in.

Jan Feb Mar Apr May Jun Jul Aug Sept Oct Nov Dec

Barn Swallow
Hirundo rustica

The graceful flight of this bird is a common summer sight. It often forages at low altitudes, so its deeply forked tail is easily observed. The Barn Swallow is actually the only swallow in San Francisco to have a 'swallow-tail.' The name 'swallow' originated in Europe, where the Barn Swallow is also common, and where it is simply called the Swallow.

The Barn Swallow builds its cup-shaped mud nests in the eaves of barns and picnic shelters, or in any other structure that provides protection from the rain. Because the Barn Swallow is often closely associated with human structures, it is not uncommon for a nervous parent bird to dive repeatedly at human 'intruders,' encouraging them to retreat.

Similar Species: Cliff Swallow (p. 95) lacks the deeply forked tail, and it has a pale forehead and a buff rump; Purple Martin (rare) has a shorter tail and lacks the russet throat and forehead.

Quick I.D.:
larger than a sparrow; deeply forked tail; glossy blue back, wings and tail; chestnut underparts; russet throat and forehead; sexes similar, but female is a bit duller.
Size: 6–8 in.

Jan Feb Mar Apr May Jun Jul Aug Sept Oct Nov Dec

Western Scrub-Jay
Aphelocoma californica

The Western Scrub-Jay is a jay of open forests, especially scrub and chaparral. You may see (and hear) the scrub-jay foraging in its characteristic manner. It frequently buries acorns by pounding them into soft soil and covering them with leaf litter or small stones. Many of the acorns are never retrieved, making scrub-jays effective dispersers for oak trees.

This is one of the few birds able to eat hairy caterpillars. A caterpillar's guard hairs are an effective defense mechanism because they irritate the digestive tracts of most birds. A scrub-jay rubs a caterpillar down in sand or soil before eating it, effectively 'shaving' off the irritating hairs. Scrub-jays also eat spiders, beetles, wasps, termites, nuts, corn, fruit, lizards and small rodents, and they visit feeders stocked with sunflower seeds, suet and peanuts.

Similar Species: Steller's Jay (p. 99) has a crest, a dark blue body and a black hood.

Quick I.D.: larger than a robin; blue head, back and tail; white throat; gray belly; long tail; no crest; sexes similar.
Size: 11–13 in.

Jan Feb Mar Apr May Jun Jul Aug Sept Oct Nov Dec

Steller's Jay
Cyanocitta stelleri

Although scarce within San Francisco's city limits, the Steller's Jay is present throughout the year in coniferous forests elsewhere around the Bay Area. With a crest unmatched by any other North American songbird and delicate blue hues sparkling in its plumage, this bird is as striking as it is extroverted and mischievous. It is less known to most North Americans than the familiar Blue Jay, and eastern birdwatchers often visit California to sight them.

Steller's Jays travel in loose flocks in August and September, and it is interesting to watch them fly directly to their destination in single-file. These jays noisily announce their arrival with their *shack-shack-shack* call. The diet of this West Coast jay is diverse: it will eat seeds, dog food and insects, and it will scavenge carcasses.

Similar Species: Western Scrub-Jay (p. 98) lacks a crest.

Quick I.D.: larger than a robin; dark crest; blue back wings and tail; black head; sexes similar.
Size: 11 in.

Jan Feb Mar Apr May Jun Jul Aug Sept Oct Nov Dec

American Crow
Corvus brachyrhynchos

The American Crow calls with the classic, long, descending *caaaw*. In late summer and fall, when their reproductive duties are completed, crows group together to roost in flocks, known as a 'murders.' For unknown reasons, the crow population has exploded in our area in recent years, and large flocks can be seen almost anywhere.

This large, black bird's intelligence has led it into many confrontations with human's, from which it often emerges the victor. Scientific studies have shown that crows are capable of solving simple problems, which comes as no surprise to anyone who has watched crows drop shellfish from the air onto rocks, cracking the shells and exposing the meaty flesh.

Similar Species: Common Raven (p. 101) is much larger and has a diamond-shaped tail.

Quick I.D.: small gull–sized; black; fan-shaped tail; slim over-all; sexes similar.
Size: 18 in.

Jan Feb Mar Apr May Jun Jul Aug Sept Oct Nov Dec

Common Raven
Corvus corax

Common Ravens are often seen gliding effortlessly on coastal updrafts over San Francisco, offering their hoarse voices to the misty air. Whether stealing food from a flock of gulls, harassing a Golden Eagle in mid-air, or confidently strutting among campers at a favorite park, the raven is worthy of its reputation as a clever bird. Glorified in traditional cultures worldwide, ravens are not restricted to the instinctive behaviors of most other birds. With the ability to express themselves playfully—tumbling aimlessly through the air or sliding down a snowy bank on their backs—these large, raucous birds flaunt traits many think of as exclusively human.

Similar Species: American Crow (p. 100) is much smaller and has a fan-shaped tail; hawks (pp. 47–50) have fan-shaped tails and are not completely black.

Quick I.D.: larger than a hawk; black; large bill; spade-shaped tail; shaggy throat; sexes similar.
In flight: spread primaries.
Size: 24 in.

Jan Feb Mar Apr May Jun Jul Aug Sept Oct Nov Dec

Chestnut-backed Chickadee
Parus rufescens

Jan Feb Mar Apr May Jun Jul Aug Sept Oct Nov Dec

Quick I.D.: smaller than a sparrow; black bib; brown cap; chestnut back; white cheek; grayish wings and tail; light underparts; faint chestnut flanks; sexes similar.
Size: 5 in.

The vivid Chestnut-backed Chickadee is most abundant in old, moist coniferous forests along the Pacific coast, where it is a year-round resident. It is also very common in Golden Gate and Lincoln parks, and it will visit backyard feeders in well-wooded neighborhoods. Even before the Chestnut-backed Chickadee is seen, its *kisssadee* call helps identify it. Small bands of birds flitting in bushes are likely to be composed of a few Chestnut-backed Chickadees in the company of Bushtits and Ruby-crowned Kinglets.

Similar Species: Townsend's Warbler (p. 119) and Black-throated Gray Warbler lack the chestnut back.

Plain Titmouse
Parus inornatus

The nasal *tsick-a-der-der* call of the Plain Titmouse is a sound of mature mixed-oak forests. These little birds are ordinary-looking, but an oak wood would seem empty without their subtle presence. The Plain Titmouse nests in natural cavities, rotted-out stumps and occasionally in abandoned woodpecker nests. It may even partially excavate a cavity in a soft decaying tree. It lines its nesting cavity with fur, moss and other soft materials.

The Plain Titmouse frequently pairs up with the same mate throughout its short life, which seldom exceeds five years. The name 'titmouse' comes from European sources: *tit* is Scandinavian for 'little,' and 'mouse' is a corruption of *mase*, the Old English word for 'bird.'

Similar Species: Bushtit (p. 104) is smaller and has a relatively longer tail; Hutton's Vireo (p. 115) has white wing bars and a faint eye-ring, and it does not have a crest.

Quick I.D.: sparrow-sized; gray-brown back, tail and wings; small crest; gray underparts; sexes similar.
Size: 5¹/₂ in.

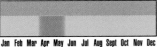

Jan Feb Mar Apr May Jun Jul Aug Sept Oct Nov Dec

Bushtit
Psaltriparus minimus

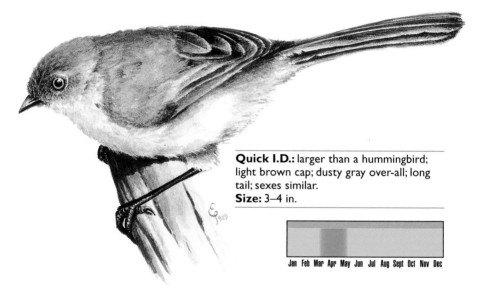

Quick I.D.: larger than a hummingbird; light brown cap; dusty gray over-all; long tail; sexes similar.
Size: 3–4 in.

Jan Feb Mar Apr May Jun Jul Aug Sept Oct Nov Dec

The character of the home reflects the quality of the occupant, and the tiny, gray Bushtit sets a fine example. The architecture of its nest is worth a close look. The intricate weaving of fine fibers, spiderwebs, grasses, mosses and lichens results in what you might mistake for an old gray sock hanging from a brushy shrub.

Their gray-brown bodies are nondescript, but Bushtits are easy to identify because of their foraging behavior: they tend to hang in every position possible while they feed. Surprisingly tiny, these tufts of continually moving feathers travel in loose flocks, appearing from dense tangles and bushes in all corners of the city. During the winter, they frequently visit backyard feeding stations, and they are very fond of suet. Bushtits often boldly approach close enough to make binoculars unnecessary.

Similar Species: Chestnut-backed Chickadee (p. 102) is larger and has a black bib; all other birds (except hummingbirds) are larger.

Pygmy Nuthatch
Sitta pygmaea

The Pygmy Nuthatch is one of the most energetic residents of Bay Area forests: it hops continuously up and down trunks and tree tops, incessantly probing and calling its high-pitched *te-dee te-dee*. Unlike other birds that forage on tree trunks, nuthatches routinely work their way down trees headfirst. Because of their unusual approach, nuthatches are capable of finding seeds and invertebrates that woodpeckers and creepers are unable to locate. The Pygmy Nuthatch is quite gregarious, and it often appears in small flocks that increase in size during the fall and winter. During winter nights, the Pygmy Nuthatch retreats to communal roosts in cavities where many birds can snuggle together.

Similar Species: White-breasted Nuthatch is larger, and it has a black crown and reddish or rusty undertail coverts; Red-breasted Nuthatch has a black eyeline and reddish underparts.

Quick I.D.: smaller than a sparrow; brownish cap bordered by dark eyeline; white cheek and throat; gray-blue back; short tail; buff-colored underparts; straight bill; sexes similar.
Size: 4–4¹/₂ in.

Jan Feb Mar Apr May Jun Jul Aug Sept Oct Nov Dec

Brown Creeper
Certhia americana

The Brown Creeper may be the most inconspicuous bird in North America. Although it is widespread in forested parks (such as Golden Gate, Tilden and Redwood), this year-round resident often goes unnoticed until a flake of bark seems to come alive.

With short, purposeful, vertical hops, the Brown Creeper spirals up a rugged trunk, constantly probing the tree's wrinkled skin for hidden insect treasures. When the spiral has reached the upper branches, the tiny bird floats down to the base of a neighboring tree to resume its foraging ascent. Only during these brief flights is the Brown Creeper easily noticed, as even their thin, faint, high-pitched *trees trees trees see the trees* whistle is too high for many birders to hear—it rarely reveals this master of concealment.

Similar Species: Woodpeckers (pp. 86–88) and nuthatches (p. 105) are more colorful.

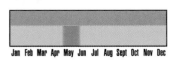

Jan Feb Mar Apr May Jun Jul Aug Sept Oct Nov Dec

Quick I.D.: smaller than a sparrow; brown back streaked with white; white breast; rusty rump; downcurved bill; long tail; sexes similar.
Size: 5 in.

Bewick's Wren
Thryomanes bewickii

The Bewick's Wren ranges throughout California. It is the most common wren in our area, especially in shrubby areas, and it prefers the undergrowth of our parks and the ornamental shrubs in our yards. These year-round singers are always more abundant than they seem to be, and they frequently nest in backyard nest boxes, natural cavities, wood piles, sheds and garages.

The mission in this wren's life appears to involve the investigation of all suspicious noises, which makes it an easy bird to attract. Their easily identifiable songs seem individualized, as though each male has added his own twist. Learning the tone and quality of the Bewick's Wren's song is the best way to find this bird.

Similar Species: Winter Wren (p. 108) and House Wren both lack the white eyebrow, and they have shorter tails; Marsh Wren (p. 109) has a streaked back and lives in marshes.

Quick I.D.: smaller than a sparrow; long, brown tail is often cocked up; white eyebrow; light throat and breast; bill slightly downcurved; tail longer than legs; sexes similar.
Size: 5–5¹/₂ in.

Jan Feb Mar Apr May Jun Jul Aug Sept Oct Nov Dec

Winter Wren
Troglodytes aedon

This common bird of parks and deep woodlands sings as though its lungs are bottomless. By following the song to its source, you may observe a Winter Wren in coastal woodlands, skulking beneath the dense understorey. Like most wrens, this year-round resident frequently carries its short tail cocked straight up.

The song of the Winter Wren is distinguished by its melodious tone and by its endurance. Although far smaller than a sparrow, the Winter Wren offers an unending song of high, tinkling warbles all in one breath. As spring arrives, the Winter Wren treats coastal residents to a few weeks of these wonderful warbles before it channels its energy into the task of reproduction.

Similar Species: Bewick's Wren (p. 107) has a white eyebrow and a much longer tail; House Wren has a much longer tail.

Quick I.D.: smaller than a sparrow; brown over-all; short tail is cocked-up; sexes similar.
Size: 4 in.

Jan Feb Mar Apr May Jun Jul Aug Sept Oct Nov Dec

Marsh Wren
Cistothorus palustris

This energetic little bird usually lives in cattail marshes and dense, wet meadows bordered by willows. Although it usually sings in the deep vegetation, its distinctive voice is one of the characteristic sounds of our freshwater wetlands. In early spring, Lake Merced and Rodeo Lagoon ring with the dynamic call of this reclusive bird. The song has the repetitive quality of an old sewing machine. Once you learn the rhythm, you will hear it whenever you visit freshwater wetlands.

A typical sighting of a Marsh Wren is spotting a brown blur moving noisily about within shoreline tangles. Although the wren may be less than 3 yards from the observer, its cryptic habits and appearance are effective camouflage. Patient observers may be rewarded with a brief glimpse of a Marsh Wren perching high atop a cattail reed as it quickly evaluates its territory.

Similar Species: Bewick's (p. 107), Winter (p. 108) and House wrens all have unstreaked backs and generally avoid wetlands.

Quick I.D.: smaller than a sparrow; brown over-all; white streaking on back; white eyeline; light throat and breast; cocked-up tail; sexes similar.
Size: 4–5 ^{1}/$_2$ in.

Jan Feb Mar Apr May Jun Jul Aug Sept Oct Nov Dec

Wrentit
Chamaea fasciata

For every Wrentit they see, Bay Area residents can expect to hear dozens more. The small secretive Wrentit's voice permeates dense chaparral and coastal scrub communities throughout our area. The distinctive, bouncy song accelerates like a ping pong ball coming to rest.

Typical Wrentit habitat consists of a nearly continuous layer of brush, with no more than a few yards of gap for the small birds to cross. These long-tailed, year-round residents breed exclusively in the Pacific coast states. They usually build their nests about 2 feet off the ground in coastal sage and coyote brush thickets, carefully concealing them from nest-robbing Western Scrub-Jays.

Similar Species: Plain Titmouse (p. 103) has a small crest, dark eyes and a relatively shorter tail; Bushtit (p. 104) is smaller and has gray unstreaked plumage; Bewick's Wren (p. 107) has a white eyebrow and light underparts; Winter Wren (p. 108) has a much shorter tail.

Jan Feb Mar Apr May Jun Jul Aug Sept Oct Nov Dec

Quick I.D.: sparrow-sized; grayish-brown plumage; long, rounded tail (often cocked up); fine chest streaks; small dark bill; yellow eyes; sexes similar.
Size: 6–6½ in.

Ruby-crowned Kinglet
Regulus calendula

These kinglets are common winter visitors to San Francisco's parks and backyards, especially among coniferous trees. They arrive in September and flit continuously through our shrubs until May. Kinglets always appear nervous, with their tails and wings flicking continuously as they hop from branch to branch in search of grubs and insect eggs.

The Ruby-crowned Kinglet is similar to the Golden-crowned Kinglet in size, habits and coloration, but it has a hidden ruby crown. 'Rubies' are heard more often then they are seen, especially prior to their spring departure (February to April). Their distinctive song starts like a motor chugging to life, and then the kinglets fire off a series of loud, rising *chewy-chewy-chewy-chewy*s. These final phrases are often the only recognizable part of the song.

Similar Species: Golden-crowned Kinglet has a black outline to the crown; Hutton's Vireo (p. 115) is larger and stouter, and it has a stubby bill; Orange-crowned Warbler (p. 117) has no wing bars.

Quick I.D.: smaller than a sparrow; plump; dark olive; white wing bars; dark tail and wings; incomplete eye-ring.
Male: red crown (infrequently seen).
Female: no red crown.
Size: 4 in.

Jan Feb Mar Apr May Jun Jul Aug Sept Oct Nov Dec

Hermit Thrush
Catharus guttatus

The Hermit Thrush is certainly one of the most beautiful songsters to inhabit Bay Area woodlands and forest floors. Its enchanting song is heard from shady coniferous forests where the understorey is scattered with shrubby nesting cover. The Hermit Thrush is confined to deep forests, such as Muir Woods, while the ethereal song of the Swainson's Thrush can be heard in wet willow and alder groves.

The Hermit Thrush's song lifts the soul with each note, and leaves a fortunate listener breathless at its conclusion. The inspiring song is heard early on spring mornings, and the Hermit Thrush is routinely the last of the daytime singers to be silenced by the night. Its song is most appreciated at dusk, when it alone offers an emotional melody to the darkening forest.

Similar Species: Swainson's Thrush has a prominent, buff eye-ring, golden-brown cheeks and a rusty-brown back; young American Robin (p. 113) lacks the uniformly brown back; Fox Sparrow (p. 128) has a conical bill.

Jan Feb Mar Apr May Jun Jul Aug Sept Oct Nov Dec

Quick I.D.: smaller than a robin; pale white eye-ring; reddish rump and tail; lightly spotted throat and breast; white belly and undertail coverts; gray flanks; sexes similar.
Size: 5–7^{1}/$_{2}$ in.

American Robin
Turdus migratorius

The American Robin's close relationship with urban areas has allowed many residents an insight into a bird's life. A robin dashing around a yard in search of worms or ripe berries is as familiar to many people as its three-part *cheerily-cheery up-cheerio* song. Robins also make up part of the emotional landscape of communities as their cheery song, their spotted young and occasionally even their deaths are experiences shared by their human neighbors.

American Robins appear to be year-round residents in San Francisco, but the bird dashing on your lawn in June may not be the same bird that shivers in February. Unnoticed by most residents, the neighborhood robins take seasonal shifts; new birds arrive from the north and east when some summer residents depart for southern climes in the fall.

Similar Species: Varied Thrush has a black mask and a breast band; immature robins can be confused with other thrushes, but robins always have at least a hint of red in the breast.

Quick I.D.: smaller than a jay; dark head, back and tail; yellow bill; striped throat; white undertail coverts.
Male: brick-red breast; darker hood.
Female: slightly more orange breast; lighter hood.
Size: 9–11 in.

Jan Feb Mar Apr May Jun Jul Aug Sept Oct Nov Dec

Western Bluebird
Sialia mexicana

Dressed with the colors of a clear summer sky on its back and the warm setting sun on its breast, the male Western Bluebird looks like a little piece of pure sky come to life. To fully appreciate this open-country specialty, try to spot a male on a crisp, clear spring morning.

The Western Bluebird has lost many of its nesting sites in natural cavities to House Sparrows and European Starlings, and to the removal of dead trees from California's agricultural areas. But concerned residents rallied for the bluebird and put up thousands of nesting boxes to compensate for the losses. The Western Bluebird population has slowly increased as a result, and the vigilant residents have been rewarded with the sight of the birds' beautiful plumage in the Californian landscape.

Similar Species: American Robin (p. 113) has a dark back; male Lazuli Bunting is smaller and has a conical bill.

Quick I.D.: smaller than a robin; white undertail coverts; thin bill.
Male: deep blue upperparts and throat; rufous-brown breast and flanks.
Female: duller, brownish-gray head and back; duller blue wings and tail; lighter chestnut breast and flanks.
Size: 7 in.

Jan Feb Mar Apr May Jun Jul Aug Sept Oct Nov Dec

Hutton's Vireo
Vireo huttoni

Quick I.D.: smaller than a sparrow; gray-green upperparts; stout bill; incomplete eyering; white wing bars; sexes similar.
Size: 5 in.

Jan Feb Mar Apr May Jun Jul Aug Sept Oct Nov Dec

In early spring, the Hutton's Vireo often sings throughout the day in never-ending triplets. The song is an oscillating *zuwee zu-woo zeeoo*, with each phrase finishing on an upbeat.

The Hutton's Vireo is a year-round resident of our oak woodlands, but it is never so common that it fails to challenge the birdwatching community. it closely resembles kinglets, a few warblers and other vireos. Persistent and patient birders who wants to see a Hutton's Vireo will succeed if they scrutinize the oak woodlands of Tilden and Redwood regional parks and Golden Gate Park.

Similar Species: Ruby-crowned Kinglet (p. 111) is smaller and has a slimmer bill; Warbling Vireo (p. 116) and Orange-crowned Warbler (p. 117) both lack wing bars.

Warbling Vireo
Vireo gilvus

The Warbling Vireo can be quite common during the summer months, but you still need to make a prolonged search before spotting this bird. Lacking any splashy field marks, the Warbling Vireo is exceedingly difficult to spot unless it moves. Searching the tree tops for this inconspicuous bird may be a literal 'pain in the neck,' but the satisfaction in visually confirming its identity can be rewarding.

The velvety voice of the Warbling Vireo contrasts sharply with its dull, nondescript plumage. The often-repeated *iggly wiggly iggly piggly iggly eeek?* song delights the listening forest with its oscillating quality. The phrases finish on an upbeat, as if the bird is asking a question of the wilds.

Similar Species: Hutton's Vireo (p. 115) has two wing bars, is much smaller and has an incomplete eye-ring; Plain Titmouse (p. 103) has a pointed crest and no eyebrow; Orange-crowned Warbler (p. 117) is smaller, its upperparts are more olive-green, and its underparts are yellowish.

Quick I.D.: smaller than a sparrow; white eyebrow; no wing bars; olive-gray upperparts; greenish flanks; light underparts; gray crown; sexes similar.
Size: 4^1/$_2$–5^1/$_2$ in.

Jan Feb Mar Apr May Jun Jul Aug Sept Oct Nov Dec

Orange-crowned Warbler
Vermivora celata

Quick I.D.: smaller than a sparrow; dusky yellow underparts; darker upperparts; faint orange crown (rarely seen); sexes similar.
Size: 4–5 in.

Jan Feb Mar Apr May Jun Jul Aug Sept Oct Nov Dec

The tinkling trill of this migrant is far more distinctive than its plumage. This bird's species name, *celata*, means 'to conceal in,' and it refers to this warbler's infrequently seen orange crown; it could just as easily refer to its unmarked dress.

The Orange-crowned Warbler is very common in the Bay Area from mid-March through August. It nests and feeds in shrubby thickets in city parks, undeveloped lands and occasionally in forested backyards, where bushes echo with their descending trill.

Similar Species: Hutton's Vireo (p. 115), Wilson's Warbler (p. 121) and Yellow Warbler all have distinctive field marks.

Yellow-rumped Warbler
Dendroica coronata

The Yellow-rumped Warbler is the Cadillac of birds—it has all the extras (wing bars, crown, breast streaks, colored rump, etc.). In the winter and during migrations, the Yellow-rumped Warbler is abundant throughout the San Francisco Bay Area, often crowding into flowing eucalyptus; during the summer this bird retreats to the mountains.

The western race of the Yellow-rumped Warbler has a glorious yellow throat. It was formerly called the Audubon's Warbler, distinguishing it from the white-throated eastern form, which was known as the Myrtle Warbler. Ironically, although the western race bore the name of one of the greatest ornithologists, it was one of the few birds that Audubon failed to meet. Although it no longer officially holds the Audubon title, many western birders continue to refer to this spry bird by its former name, affirming its western roots.

Similar Species: Townsend's Warbler (p. 119) and Black-throated Gray Warbler both lack the combination of a yellow rump and whitish underparts; eastern Yellow-rumped Warbler (Myrtle Warbler) has a white throat and occurs mostly in wetter habitats.

Quick I.D.: smaller than a sparrow; blue-black back, tail and wings; yellow rump, shoulder patches and crown; yellow throat; white wing bars; dark chest band; white belly; dark cheek. *Male:* bright colors. *Female:* less intense colors. **Size:** 6 in.

Jan Feb Mar Apr May Jun Jul Aug Sept Oct Nov Dec

Townsend's Warbler
Dendroica townsendi

The Townsend's Warbler lives high up in trees. Its bold colors, flitting habits and unmistakable *weezy weezy weezy weezy tweee* song help to distinguish it from other warblers. Many species of warbler can coexist in our coniferous forests because they partition the food supplies by foraging exclusively in certain areas of the trees.

The Townsend's Warbler breeds at higher elevations (above 2000 feet) in the Cascades and Olympics of Oregon and Washington, but they are easily found in the lowlands around San Francisco during migration and through the winter. Many Townsend's Warblers winter in San Francisco, flocking together with chickadees and nuthatches, adding a splash of color and sound to the lively winter scene.

Similar Species: Black-throated Gray Warbler lacks the yellow plumage; Hermit Warbler (uncommon in San Francisco) lacks the black cheek patch.

Quick I.D.: smaller than a sparrow; black throat; yellow face; dark cheek patch; olive back; dark wings and tail; white wing bars. *Male:* larger black bib.
Size: 5 in.

Jan Feb Mar Apr May Jun Jul Aug Sept Oct Nov Dec

Common Yellowthroat
Geothlypis trichas

The male of this energetic wetland warbler is easily identified by his black mask or by his oscillating *witchety-witchety-witchety* song. In our area, the Common Yellowthroat reaches its highest abundance along the wetland brambles and cattails of Lake Merced and at Rodeo Lagoon, but it can be seen and heard along the vegetation bordering many freshwater bodies.

Female yellowthroats are rarely seen because they keep their nests deep within the thick vegetation surrounding marshes. The Common Yellowthroat's nests are often parasitized by Brown-headed Cowbirds. Since cowbirds are principally birds of the open country, they commonly target the nests of birds that do not nest in deep forests, such as Common Yellowthroats, Yellow Warblers, Red-eyed Vireos and Song Sparrows.

Similar Species: Male is distinct; female Nashville Warbler (rare in San Francisco) has dark brown legs.

Jan Feb Mar Apr May Jun Jul Aug Sept Oct Nov Dec

Quick I.D.: smaller than a sparrow; orange legs; yellow throat and underparts; olive upperparts.
Male: black mask, with white border on forehead.
Female: no mask.
Size: 4¹/₂–5¹/₂ in.

Wilson's Warbler
Wilsonia pusilla

The hearty chatter of the Wilson's Warbler reveals the presence of this small, colorful bird. It feeds energetically on caterpillars and other insects in branches that are low to the ground, often near water. Often flitting to within a branch of onlookers, this energetic warbler bounces from one perch to another like an overwound wind-up toy.

This warbler was named for Alexander Wilson, the father of American ornithology. During its spring and fall migrations, the Wilson's Warbler can be found almost anywhere in San Francisco, including well-planted backyards. During the nesting season, however, it becomes far more discriminating and secretive, and it cautiously conceals its nest site.

Similar Species: Orange-crowned Warbler (p. 117) has greener plumage and lacks the black cap; Yellow Warbler has a streaked breast and lacks the black cap.

Quick I.D.: smaller than a sparrow; lemon-yellow underparts; olive to dark green upperparts.
Male: black cap.
Female: duller cap.
Size: 5 in.

Jan Feb Mar Apr May Jun Jul Aug Sept Oct Nov Dec

Northern Mockingbird
Mimus polyglottos

Quick I.D.: robin-sized; white patches in black wings and tail; gray head and back; light underparts; long tail; thin bill; sexes similar.
Size: 10 in.

Jan Feb Mar Apr May Jun Jul Aug Sept Oct Nov Dec

Once largely restricted to desert scrub and chaparral in southern California, the Northern Mockingbird is now a common sight in San Francisco. Mockingbirds followed agricultural and urban development northward, and they were first noticed in the Bay Area in around 1928. Since then, these common urban birds have adapted well to the broken forests and urban fruit-bearing bushes so common in our region.

The Northern Mockingbird is perhaps best known for its ability to mimic sounds. It can expertly imitate other birds, barking dogs and even musical instruments. So accurate is the mimicry that sonographic analysis often cannot detect differences between the original version and the mockingbird's.

Similar Species: Loggerhead Shrike has a black mask and a stout, hooked bill.

Cedar Waxwing
Bombycilla cedrorum

A faint, high-pitched trill is often your first clue that waxwings are around. Search the treetops to see these cinnamon-crested birds as they dart out in quick bursts, snacking on flying insects. Cedar Waxwings are found in many habitats throughout the Bay Area, wherever ripe berries provide abundant food supplies.

Cedar Waxwings are most often seen in large flocks in late spring, when they congregate on fruit trees and quickly eat all the berries. Some people remember these visits not only for the birds' beauty, but because fermentation of the fruit occasionally renders the flock flightless from intoxication.

Similar Species: Plain Titmouse (p. 103) has no yellow on its belly or tail.

Quick I.D.: smaller than a robin; fine, pale brown plumage; small crest; black mask; yellow belly wash; yellow-tipped tail; light undertail coverts; shiny red (waxy-looking) droplets on wingtips; sexes similar.
Size: 8 in.

Jan Feb Mar Apr May Jun Jul Aug Sept Oct Nov Dec

European Starling
Sturnus vulgaris

In 1942, 52 years after their intentional release in New York's Central Park, European Starlings began to establish themselves in California. Less than a decade later, flocks of over 1 million birds were being reported. Today, European Starlings are one of the most common birds in the San Francisco area. Their presence is highlighted by astonishing numbers roosting communally during the winter months.

Unfortunately, the expansion of starlings has come at the expense of many of our native birds, including the Purple Martin and the Western Bluebird, which are unable to defend nest cavities against the aggressive starling. While not all birdwatchers are pleased with the presence of this foreigner to our area, starlings have become a permanent fixture in the bird community. If residents are unable to find joy in this bird's mimicry and flocking, they may take some comfort from the fact that starlings now provide a reliable and stable food source for woodland hawks and the Peregrine Falcon.

Similar Species: All blackbirds (pp. 133–35) have long tails and black bills; Purple Martin has a short bill.

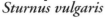

Quick I.D.: smaller than a robin; short tail; sexes similar.
Breeding: dark, glossy plumage; long, yellow bill.
Non-breeding: dark bill; spotty plumage.
Juvenile: brown upperparts; gray-brown underparts; brown bill.
Size: 9 in.

Jan Feb Mar Apr May Jun Jul Aug Sept Oct Nov Dec

Black-headed Grosbeak
Pheucticus melanocephalus

The male Black-headed Grosbeak has a brilliant voice to match his Halloween plumage, and he flaunts his song in treetop performances. This common songster's boldness does not go unnoticed by the appreciative birding community, which eagerly anticipates the male's annual spring concert. The female lacks the formal dress, but she shares her partner's musical talents. Whether the nest is tended by the male or female, the developing young are continually introduced into the world of song by the brooding parent.

This neotropical migrant nests in mature deciduous forests, such as those found in parts of Tilden and Redwood regional parks or in less developed urban areas.

Similar Species: Spotted Towhee (p. 126) has a smaller bill and a longer tail; female Purple Finch and female sparrows (pp. 128–31) are generally smaller.

Quick I.D.: smaller than a robin; light-colored, conical bill. *Male:* black head, wings and tail; orange body; white wing patches. *Female:* finely streaked with brown; white eyebrow; light throat.
Size: 7–8¹/₂ in.

Jan Feb Mar Apr May Jun Jul Aug Sept Oct Nov Dec

Spotted Towhee
Pipilo maculatus

This large, colorful sparrow is most often heard before it is seen, scratching away leaves and debris in the dense understorey. It is a common year-round resident in many Bay Area parks and shrubby backyards. Deep in the shadows of shrubs, the Spotted Towhee's sharp, nasal *t'wee* identifies this secretive sparrow.

To best observe this bird, which was formerly grouped with the Eastern Towhee (together they were known as the Rufous-sided Towhee), learn a few birding tricks. Squeaking and pishing are irresistible for towhees, which will quickly pop out from the cover to investigate the curious noise.

Similar Species: American Robin (p. 113) is larger and has no white on its chest; Black-headed Grosbeak (p. 125) has an orange chest, a larger bill and a shorter tail; Dark-eyed Junco (p. 132) is smaller and has white outer tail feathers.

Jan Feb Mar Apr May Jun Jul Aug Sept Oct Nov Dec

Quick I.D.: smaller than a robin; black head; rufous-colored flanks; spotted back; white outer tail feathers; white underparts; red eyes.
Male: black head, breast and upperparts.
Female: reddish-brown head, breast and upperparts.
Size: 9 in.

California Towhee
Pipilo crissalis

The sharp metallic *chip* note of the California Towhee bursts from Bay Area bushes and shrubs in a proclamation of this bird's territory. California Towhees are strongly territorial, and in the dense vegetation of backyards, city parks, coastal scrub and broken chaparral communities, pairs establish and aggressively defend their territories against their neighbors.

California Towhees are year-round residents in the Bay Area and they may build their nests in well-vegetated parks and backyards. These woodland-edge specialists build their bulky nests fairly low to the ground in a bush. They peck and scratch for seeds on the bare ground in open areas, and if a pair is separated while foraging, they re-establish contact by squealing atop a bush. Once reunited, they bob rhythmically to reaffirm their life-long bond.

Until recently, the California Towhee and the Canyon Towhee were lumped together (and known as the Brown Towhee), but recent studies have shown that the birds living in lowland California are a separate species.

Similar Species: Female Brewer's Blackbird (p. 134) lacks the rusty undertail coverts and the conical bill; California Thrasher has a long curved bill, a white throat and a light eyebrow.

Quick I.D.: robin-sized; brown upperparts; light brown underparts; rusty undertail coverts; brown crown; buffy throat with a broken, black necklace; short, stout, conical bill; yellow legs; long tail; sexes similar.
Juvenile: streaked underparts.
Size: 8¹/₂–10 in.

Jan Feb Mar Apr May Jun Jul Aug Sept Oct Nov Dec

Fox Sparrow
Passerella iliaca

The Fox Sparrow is a winter visitor in San Francisco's thickets and brambles; it is most common from October through April. Like many other sparrows that winter in this habitat, the Fox Sparrow is appreciated for its voice more than for its plumage. Although the subtlety of the Fox Sparrow's plumage is beautiful, its voice overshadows its appearance. During late winter, sit and wait near tangles and brush piles in San Francisco's parks, and listen as the Fox Sparrow repeatedly belts out its distinctive musical question: *all I have is what's here dear, will-you-will-you take-it?*

Similar Species: Song Sparrow (p. 129) has a different song and a much lighter color; Hermit Thrush (p. 112) has a smaller bill and thinner breast spots; Swainson's Thrush has a pale eye-ring and olive upperparts; Lincoln's Sparrow has weaker breast streaks.

Quick I.D.: large sparrow; heavy breast streaks form dark chest; brown plumage; very dark over-all; sexes similar.
Size: 6¹/₂–7 in.

Jan Feb Mar Apr May Jun Jul Aug Sept Oct Nov Dec

Song Sparrow
Melospiza melodia

The Song Sparrow's drab, heavily streaked plumage doesn't prepare you for its symphonic song, which stands among those of the great San Francisco songsters in complexity and rhythm. This commonly heard bird seems to be singing *hip-hip-hip hooray boys, the spring is here again.*

This year-round resident is encountered in a wide variety of habitats: Song Sparrows are easily found in all seasons among marshes, thickets, blackberry brambles, weedy fields and woodland edges. Although these birds are most easily identified by their grayish streaks while perched, flying birds will characteristically pump their tails.

Similar Species: Fox Sparrow (p. 128) is very heavily streaked and has a different song; Savannah Sparrow and Lincoln's Sparrow have weaker breast streaks.

Quick I.D.: mid-sized sparrow; heavy breast streaks form central chest spot; brown-red plumage; striped head; sexes similar.
Size: 6 in.

Jan Feb Mar Apr May Jun Jul Aug Sept Oct Nov Dec

White-crowned Sparrow
Zonotrichia leucophrys

White-crowned Sparrows are usually seen foraging on the ground or in low shrubs. They normally feed a short distance from thickets and tall grasses, always maintaining a quick escape path into the safety of concealing vegetation. Overwintering White-crowned Sparrows often feed at backyard feeders.

These common year-round residents of the northern California coastline represent a distinct subspecies of the White-crowned Sparrow. San Francisco's White-crowns tend to have white lores, brown upperparts and gray-brown underparts. From early spring through fall, each small population sings a unique song dialect; one population in the San Francisco area sings *I-I-I-I gotto go wee wee wee now* from the tops of bushes. White-crowns are very persistent singers, and their songs can be heard well into San Francisco's nights.

Similar Species: Golden-crowned Sparrow (p. 131) has a golden-yellow crown; White-throated Sparrow (uncommon in San Francisco) has yellow lores and a clear white throat.

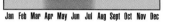

Jan Feb Mar Apr May Jun Jul Aug Sept Oct Nov Dec

Quick I.D.: large sparrow; striped, black-and-white crown; pink bill; unstreaked breast; yellow wing edge; brown upperparts; gray-brown underparts; sexes similar.
Immature: no crown; buffy-olive upperparts; faint yellow underparts.
Size: 5¹/₂–7 in.

Golden-crowned Sparrow
Zonotrichia atricapilla

Quick I.D.: large sparrow; golden-yellow crown; thick black eyebrow extending all around head; gray cheek; unstreaked breast; sexes similar. *Immature:* light streaking on head; often faint yellow forehead. **Size:** 7 in.

Jan Feb Mar Apr May Jun Jul Aug Sept Oct Nov Dec

The Golden-crowned Sparrow's *oh, dear me!* song can be heard from dense thickets and brush piles across the West Coast during its spring migration. This western sparrow is striking, with broad black eyebrows capped in gold.

On a crisp October morning, Golden Gate Park, Tilden Regional Park and Rodeo Lagoon are some of the best places to watch Golden-crowned Sparrows fly from bush to bush. During the winter months, many visit backyards, picking up and eating bird seed that has been dropped to the ground from raised feeders.

Similar Species: White-crowned Sparrow (p. 130) and White-throated Sparrow both lack the yellow crown.

Dark-eyed Junco
Junco hyemalis

While Americans east of the Rockies do have Dark-eyed Juncos, only West Coast residents have the splashy race with the black hood and tail and the pinkish body, which is sometimes called the Oregon Junco.

Many Dark-eyed Juncos breed in city parks, and they are abundant winter visitors throughout the San Francisco area. The Dark-eyed Junco is a ground dweller, and it is frequently seen as it flushes from the undergrowth along wooded trails in San Francisco's parks. The distinctive white outer tail feathers will flash in alarm as it flies down a narrow path before disappearing into a thicket. The junco's distinctive smacking call and its habit of double-scratching at forest litter also help identify it. Juncos are common guests at birdfeeders, and they usually pick up the scraps that have fallen to the ground.

Similar Species: Spotted Towhee (p. 126) is larger and has white 'flaking' on its back; Brown-headed Cowbird (p. 135) lacks the white outer tail feathers.

Jan Feb Mar Apr May Jun Jul Aug Sept Oct Nov Dec

Quick I.D.: mid-sized sparrow; black hood; brown back; pinkish sides; pink bill; white outer tail feathers; white belly; sexes similar.
Size: 5–6¹/₂ in.

Red-winged Blackbird
Agelaius phoeniceus

From March through July, no marsh is free from the loud calls and bossy, aggressive nature of the Red-winged Blackbird. A springtime walk around Lake Merced or through the brush at Rodeo Lagoon will be accompanied by this bird's loud, raspy and persistent *konk-a-reee* or *eat my CHEEEzies* song.

The male's bright red shoulders are his most important tool in the strategic and intricate displays he uses to defend his territory from rivals and to attract a mate. In experiments, males whose red shoulders were painted black soon lost their territories to rivals they had previously defeated. The female's interest lies not in the individual combatants, but in nesting habitat, and a male who can successfully defend a large area of dense cattails will breed with many females. After the females have built their concealed nests and laid their eggs, the male continues his persistent vigil.

Similar Species: Brewer's Blackbird (p. 134) and Brown-headed Cowbird (p. 135) both lack the red shoulder patches; Tricolored Blackbird has dark red shoulder patches with white trim.

Quick I.D.: smaller than a robin.
Male: all-black plumage; large red patch on each shoulder.
Female: brown over-all; heavily streaked; hint of red on shoulder.
Size: 7¹/₂–9¹/₂ in.

Jan Feb Mar Apr May Jun Jul Aug Sept Oct Nov Dec

Brewer's Blackbird
Euphagus cyanocephalus

These small blackbirds are common at Cliff House and Golden Gate Park, where they squabble with pigeons and starlings for leftover scraps of food. In the San Francisco Bay Area, this species is most abundant in rural pastureland, in river valleys and along highways, where they are observed strutting confidently in defiance of nearby, rapidly moving vehicles.

Brewer's Blackbirds are bold, and they allow us to easily and intimately observe them. By studying the behavior of several birds within a flock, you can determine the hierarchy of the flock as it is perceived by the birds themselves. Brewer's Blackbird feathers, which superficially appear black, actually show an iridescent quality as reflected rainbows of sunlight move along the feather shafts.

Similar Species: Male Red-winged Blackbird (p. 133) has a red patch on each wing; male Brown-headed Cowbird (p. 135) has a brown hood; female and immature Brown-headed Cowbirds have shorter tails and stout bills.

Jan Feb Mar Apr May Jun Jul Aug Sept Oct Nov Dec

Quick I.D.: robin-sized; long tail; slim bill. *Male:* all-black, slightly iridescent plumage; light yellow eyes. *Female:* brown over-all; brown eyes. **Size:** 8–10 in.

Brown-headed Cowbird
Molothrus ater

Since it first arrived in the San Francisco area in 1922, the Brown-headed Cowbird has firmly established itself within the matrix of the region's bird life. This gregarious bird is very common in city parks during the summer months. During the winter, it commonly mixes with other black-birds in outlying agricultural areas, and it can be seen at Lake Merced and Cliff House.

The Brown-headed Cowbird is infamous for being a nest parasite—female cowbirds do not incubate their own eggs, but instead lay them in the nests of many songbirds. Cowbird eggs have a short incubation period, and the cowbird chicks often hatch before the host songbird's own chicks. Many songbirds do not recognize that the fast-growing cowbird chick is not one of their own, and they will continue to feed it even after the cowbird chick has grown larger than the songbird. In its efforts to get as much food as possible, a cowbird chick may squeeze the host's own young out of the nest. The populations of some songbirds have been reduced in part by the activities of the Brown-headed Cowbird, but other songbird species recognize the foreign egg, and they either eject it from their nest or they build a new nest.

Similar Species: Male Brewer's Blackbird (p. 134) has a purple head and a yellow eye; female Brewer's Blackbird has a long tail and a thin bill.

Quick I.D.: smaller than a robin. *Male:* metallic-looking, glossy black plumage; soft brown head; dark eyes. *Female:* brownish gray over-all; dark eye; slight chest streaks.
Size: 6–8 in.

Jan Feb Mar Apr May Jun Jul Aug Sept Oct Nov Dec

Western Meadowlark
Sturnella neglecta

Although a few Western Meadowlarks breed in grasslands around the San Francisco area, the occurrence of this open-country bird is most notable during the winter months. Their fiercely defended summer solitude and territoriality is abandoned in the winter, and flocks of up to 40 meadowlarks can be seen wheeling over open fields, pastures and river deltas, taking off and alighting in unison.

The Western Meadowlark is well adapted to wide open spaces: its long legs carry it quickly through the grass, and its mottled color blends in with the often drab surroundings. In anticipation of their spring departure, Western Meadowlarks may begin singing in March, offering up their melodies to the fields in which they wintered.

Similar Species: None.

Quick I.D.: robin-sized; mottled brown upperparts; black 'V' on chest; yellow throat and belly; white outer tail feathers; striped head; sexes similar.
Size: 8–10 in.

Jan Feb Mar Apr May Jun Jul Aug Sept Oct Nov Dec

House Finch
Carpodacus mexicanus

The House Finch is one of the earliest voices to announce the coming of spring. These common city and country birds sing their melodies from backyards, parks, ivy vines and telephone lines.

During the 1920s and 1930s, these birds, native to the American Southwest, were popular cage birds, and they were sold across the continent as Hollywood Finches. Illegal releases of the caged birds and expansion from their historic range have resulted in two separate distributions in North America, which have recently converged.

Similar Species: Male Purple Finch is raspberry-colored and has unstreaked undertail coverts; female Purple Finch has a brown cheek contrasting with a white eyebrow and a mustache stripe.

Quick I.D.: sparrow-sized; squared tail.
Male: deep red forehead, eyebrow and throat; buffy streaked belly; brown cheek; streaked undertail coverts.
Female: brown over-all; streaked underparts; brown face; no eyebrow.
Size: 5–5¹/₂ in.

Jan Feb Mar Apr May Jun Jul Aug Sept Oct Nov Dec

American Goldfinch
Carduelis tristis

Quick I.D.: smaller than a sparrow.
Breeding male: black forehead, wings and tail; canary-yellow body; wings show white in flight.
Female and *Non-breeding male:* no black on forehead; yellow-green over-all; black wings and tail.

Jan Feb Mar Apr May Jun Jul Aug Sept Oct Nov Dec

Size: 4¹/₂–5¹/₂ in.

In the spring, the American Goldfinch swings over fields in its distinctive, undulating flight, and it fills the air with its jubilant *po-ta-to chip!* call. This bright, cheery songbird is commonly seen during the summer in weedy fields, roadsides and backyards, where it often feeds on thistle seeds. The American Goldfinch delays nesting until June or July to ensure a dependable source of insects, thistles and dandelion seeds to feed its young.

The American Goldfinch is a common backyard bird in parts of the Bay Area, and it can easily be attracted to feeding stations that offer a supply of niger seed. Unfortunately, goldfinches are easily bullied at feeders by larger sparrows and finches. Only goldfinches and Pine Siskins invert for food, however, so a special finch feeder with openings below the perches is ideal for ensuring a steady stream of these 'wild canaries.'

Similar Species: Evening Grosbeak is much larger; Wilson's Warbler (p. 121) and Yellow Warbler do not have black on their forehead or wings.

Pine Siskin
Carduelis pinus

Tight, wheeling flocks of these gregarious birds are frequently heard before they are seen. Their characteristic call—*zzzweeet*—starts off slowly and then climbs to a high-pitched climax. Once you recognize this distinctive call, a flurry of activity in the treetops, showing occasional flashes of yellow, will confirm the presence of Pine Siskins.

The Pine Siskin is a year-round, but unpredictable, resident in San Francisco, and in all seasons it can be found in moist conifer stands in most of the larger parks. Occasionally, flocks descend into weedy fields and shrubby areas, where siskins use their pointed bills to extract the seeds of red alder and thistles in the fall.

Similar Species: Fox Sparrow (p. 128), Song Sparrow (p. 129), female finches (p. 137) and female crossbills all lack the yellow wing and tail linings.

Quick I.D.:
smaller than a sparrow; lightly streaked underparts; yellow flashes in wings and tail; streaked brown upperparts; sexes similar.
Size: 5 in.

Jan Feb Mar Apr May Jun Jul Aug Sept Oct Nov Dec

House Sparrow
Passer domesticus

This common backyard bird often confuses novice birdwatchers because females and immatures can be very nondescript. The male is relatively conspicuous—he has a black bib, a gray cap and white lines trailing down from his mouth (as though he has spilled milk on himself)—and he sings a continuous series of *cheep-cheep-cheeps*. The best field mark for the female, apart from her pale eyebrows, is that there are no distinctive field marks.

The House Sparrow was introduced to North America in the 1850s to control insects. Although this familiar bird can consume great quantities of insects, the majority of its diet is seeds, and it has become somewhat of a pest. The House Sparrow's aggressive nature usurps several native songbirds from nesting cavities, and its boldness often drives other birds away from backyard feeders. The House Sparrow and the European Starling are now two of the most common birds in cities and on farms, and they are a constant reminder of the negative impact of human introductions on natural systems.

Similar Species: Male is distinctive; female is similar to female sparrows (pp. 128–31) and female finches (p. 137).

Quick I.D.: mid-sized sparrow; brownish-gray belly.
Male: black throat; gray forehead; white jowls; chestnut nape.
Female: plain; pale eyebrow; mottled wings.
Size: 5¹/₂–6¹/₂ in.

Jan Feb Mar Apr May Jun Jul Aug Sept Oct Nov Dec

Watching Birds

Identifying your first new bird can be so satisfying that you just might become addicted to birdwatching. Luckily, birdwatching does not have to be expensive. It all hinges on how involved in this hobby you want to get. Setting up a simple backyard feeder is an easy way to get to know the birds sharing your neighborhood, and some people simply find birdwatching a pleasant way to complement a nightly walk with the dog or a morning commute into work.

Many people enjoy going to urban parks and feeding the wild birds that have become accustomed to humans. This activity provides people with intimate contact with urban-dwelling birds, but remember that birdseed, or better yet the birds' natural food items, are much healthier for the birds than bread and crackers. As a spokesperson for the animals' health, kindly remind 'bread tossers' of the implications of their actions.

SEASONS OF BIRDWATCHING

Spring

A calendar indicates the arrival of spring around March 21st, but for birdwatchers, the changing season is indicated by migration and bird songs. One brisk morning in February, a Ruby-crowned Kinglet, House Finch or Winter Wren will suddenly decide to sing. After an eight-month absence the music begins slowly, but within a month the infectious desire to sing strikes most coastal songbirds. Coinciding with the musical upsurge, Barn Swallows from southern retreats grace the skies, and migrant sparrows investigate brambles and shrubs. Coastal activities mirror those inland, as overwintering loons, grebes and waterfowl trickle away to their northern breeding grounds.

Brant pass through, followed by clouds of 'wind birds' (sandpipers and plovers). Shorebirds descend in uncountable flocks, coating mudflats and rich shorelines in soul-tickling scenes. Soon the beaches are empty, and the forests no longer ring with a multitude of songs. It is time for the serious business of nesting.

Summer

Summertime finds birds busy with their nesting and less likely to put on shows for human observers. Singing gives way to nest-building and incubation. Once the chicks are born, the parents are kept busy feeding the insatiable young. Summer can be extremely enjoyable for San Francisco residents who have set out nest boxes. Watching the birds' reproductive cycles, from breeding to fledging, can provide some memorable experiences. Long, warm days invite us into nature's realm and offer opportunities to visit nearby state and national parks. It is during these excursions that most memorable bird encounters are experienced.

Fall

The fall migration through San Francisco is not as focused as that of the spring, but it is not as rushed either, and the fall migration season tends to last months instead of weeks. Geographical features once again funnel birds across the state, with periodic concentrations gathering along the shorelines of San Francisco Bay. Small flocks are often silent, and they lack the vivid colors of their springtime surge. Fall flocks often include birds of several different species; in the spring the birds are most focused on their own species. Migrant species disappear slowly, their numbers gently trickling out with the coming of the cold.

Winter

Far from the desolate landscape that enslaves inland birdwatching communities, San Francisco remains a haven for birds in the winter. Mild weather attract thousands of waterbirds. Occasional irruptions of finches may descend on backyard feeders to join the more habitual winter jays, juncos and chickadees. Winter is a time for birdfeeders, and a productive yard may reveal a surprising diversity of species. It is also at this time of year that the birdwatcher can arrange field notes and photos, and plan upcoming trips for the spring. But take care not to overlook the wintering birds: their resilience and fortitude are most enviable on crisp mornings.

BIRDING OPTICS

Most people who are interested in birdwatching will eventually buy a pair of binoculars. They help you identify key bird characteristics, such as plumage and bill color, and they also help you identify other birders! Birdwatchers are a friendly sort, and a chat among birders is all part of the experience.

You'll use your binoculars often, so select a pair that will contribute to the quality of your birdwatching experience—they don't have to be expensive. If you need help deciding which pair would be right for you, talk to other birdwatchers or to someone at your local nature center. Many models are available, and when shopping for binoculars it's important to keep two things in mind: weight and magnification.

One of the first things you'll notice about binoculars (apart from the price extremes) is that they all have two numbers associated with them (8x40, for example). The first number, which is always the smallest, is the magnification (how large the bird will appear), while the second is the size (in millimeters) of the objective lens (the larger end). It may seem important at first to get the highest magnification possible, but a reasonable magnification of 7x–8x is optimal for all-purpose birding, because it draws you fairly close to most birds without causing too much shaking. Some shaking happens to everyone; to overcome it, rest the binoculars against a support, such as a partner's shoulder or a tree.

The size of the objective lens is really a question of birding conditions and weight. Because wider lenses (40–50 mm) will bring in more light, these are preferred for birding in low-light situations (like before sunrise or after sunset). If these aren't the conditions that you will be pursuing, a light pair that has an objective lens diameter of less than 30 mm may be the right choice. Because binoculars tend to become heavy after hanging around your neck all day, the compact models are becoming increasingly popular. If you have a pair that is heavy, you can purchase a strap that redistributes part of the weight to the shoulders and lower back.

Another valuable piece of equipment is a spotting scope. It is very useful when you are trying to sight waterfowl, shorebirds or soaring raptors, but it is really of no use if you are intent on seeing forest birds. A good spotting scope has a magnification of around 40x. It has a sturdy tripod or a window mount for the car. Be wary of second-hand models of telescopes, as they are designed for seeing stars, and their magnification is too great for birdwatching. One of the advantages of having a scope is that you will be able to see far-off birds, which can help during Seattle's winters (to see overwintering waterfowl and alcids) or during migration (to see shorebirds and raptors). By setting up in one spot (or by not even leaving your car) you can observe faraway flocks that would be little more than specks in your binoculars.

With these simple pieces of equipment (none of which is truly essential) and this handy field guide, anyone can enjoy birds in their area. Many birds are difficult to see because they stay hidden in treetops, but you can learn to identify them by their songs. After experiencing the thrill of a couple of hard-won identifications, you will find yourself taking your binoculars on walks, drives and trips to the beach and cabin. As rewards accumulate with experience, you may find the books and photos piling up and your trips being planned just to see birds!

BIRDING BY EAR

Sometimes, bird listening can be more effective than bird watching. The technique of birding by ear is gaining popularity, because listening for birds can be more efficient, productive and rewarding than waiting for a visual confirmation. Birds have distinctive songs that they use to resolve territorial disputes, and sound is therefore a useful way to identify species. It is particularly useful when trying to watch some of the smaller forest-dwelling birds. Their size and often indistinct plumage can make a visual search of the forest canopy frustrating. To facilitate auditory searches, catchy paraphrases are included in the descriptions of many of the birds. If the paraphrase just doesn't seem to work for you (they are often a personal thing) be creative and try to find one that fits. By spending time playing the song over in your head, fitting words to it, the voices of birds soon become as familiar as the voices of family members. Many excellent CDs and tapes are available at bookstores and wild-bird stores for the songs of the birds in your area.

KEEPING BIRD NOTES

Although most naturalists realize the usefulness of keeping accurate and concise notes of their observations, few are proud of their written records. It's easy to become overwhelmed by the excitement in the field and forget to jot down a few quick observations.

It's a good idea for every level of birdwatcher to get into the habit of carrying a soft, small notebook in a pocket or backpack. For the novice who is unsure of a bird's identity, a quick sketch (using a pencil is best), and a description of the bird's behavior and habits will help to confirm your sightings later. A simple line sketch is ideal, and it really doesn't matter how artistic it is! For more experienced birdwatchers, the activities of an observed bird and the dates on which it was seen can be accumulated over time as an ongoing personal study.

If you don't want to bother with a notebook, try a small, compact tape recorder to record field observations. The advantages of this method are its quickness and its usefulness in recording unfamiliar bird calls. By recording observations and calls, your field notes can be compiled at a later time in an unhurried manner.

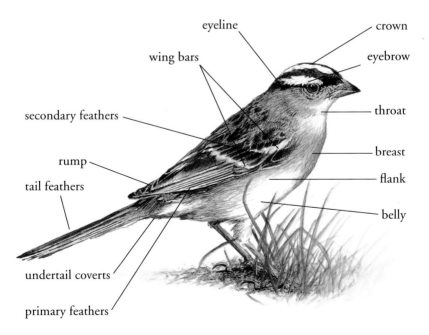

A notebook provides an excellent way to remember and relive the moment in the field at a later time. A comprehensive notebook can even provide information to researchers who are looking at the dynamics of birds. Even keeping a count of feeder birds over a period of years can help ornithologists with their understanding of population ecology.

Another good way to learn about birds is to join your local Audubon or bird society. You will meet many knowledgeable people who will be glad to teach you what they know about birds, and to show you the best places to see them. Many organizations run field trips to some of the good bird-watching spots, and they provide the benefit of an expert to help with identification problems. Christmas Bird Counts are a highlight for bird-watchers, regardless of skill level. Look for information on these in your local paper.

BIRDFEEDERS

They're messy, they can be costly, and they're sprouting up in neighborhoods everywhere. Feeding birds has become a common pastime in residential communities all over North America. Although the concept is fairly straightforward, as with anything else involving birds, feeders can become quite elaborate.

The great advantage to feeding birds is that neighborhood chickadees, jays, juncos and finches are enticed into regular visits. Don't expect birds to arrive at your feeder as soon as you set it up; it may take weeks for a few regulars to incorporate your yard into their daily routine. As the popularity of your feeder grows, the number of visiting birds will increase and more species will arrive. You will notice that your feeder is busier during the winter months, when natural foods are less abundant. You can increase the odds of a good avian turnout by using a variety of feeders and seeds. When a number of birds habitually visit your yard, maintaining the food source becomes a responsibility because they may have begun to rely on your feeder as a regular source of food.

Larger birds tend to enjoy feeding on platforms or on the ground, while smaller birds are comfortable on hanging seed dispensers. Certain seeds tend to attract specific birds; nature centers and wild-bird supply stores are the best places to ask how to attract a favorite species. It's mainly seed eaters that are attracted to backyards—some birds have no interest in feeders. Only the most committed birdwatcher will try to attract birds that are insect eaters, berry eaters, or, in some extreme cases, scavengers!

The location of the feeder may influence the amount of business it receives from the neighborhood birds. Because birds are wild, they are wary, and they are unlikely to visit an area where they may come under attack. When putting up your feeder, think like a bird. A good clear view with convenient escape routes is always appreciated. Cats like birdfeeders that are close to the ground and within pouncing distance from a bush; obviously, birds don't. Above all, a birdfeeder should be in view of a favorite window, where you can sit and enjoy the rewarding interaction of your appreciative feathered guests.

Glossary

accipiter: a forest hawk (genus *Accipiter*); characterized by a long tail and short, rounded wings; feeds mostly on birds.

alcid: a seabird of the auk family (Alcidae); includes auks, murres, puffins and guillemots.

brood: *n.* a family of young from one hatching; *v.* sit on eggs so as to hatch them.

coniferous: cone-producing trees, usually softwood evergreens (e.g., spruce, pine, fir).

corvid: a member of the crow family (Corvidae); includes crows, jays, magpies and ravens.

covey: a brood or flock of partridges, quail or grouse.

crop: an enlargement of the esophagus, serving as a storage structure and (in pigeons) has glands which produce secretions.

cryptic: coloration that blends with the environment.

dabbling: foraging technique used by ducks, where the head and neck are submerged but the body and tail remain on the water's surface.

dabbling duck: a duck that forages by dabbling; it can usually walk easily on land, it can take off without running, and it has a brightly colored speculum; includes Mallards, Gadwalls, teals and others.

deciduous: a tree that loses its leaves annually (e.g., oak, maple, aspen, birch).

dimorphism: the existence of two distinct forms of a species, such as between the sexes.

eclipse: the dull, female-like plumage that male ducks briefly acquire after molting from their breeding plumage.

elbow patches: dark spots at the bend of the outstretched wing, seen from below.

flycatching: feeding behavior where a bird leaves a perch, snatches an insect in mid-air, and returns to their previous perch; also known as 'hawking' or 'sallying.'

fledgling: a young chick that has just acquired its permanent flight feathers, but is still dependent on its parents.

flushing: a behavior where frightened birds explode into flight in response to a disturbance.

gape: the size of the mouth opening.

invertebrate: an animal that lacks a backbone or vertebral column (e.g., insects, spiders, mollusks, worms).

irruption: a sporadic mass migration of birds into a non-breeding area.

larva: a development stage of an animal (usually an invertebrate) that has a different body form from the adult (e.g., caterpillar, maggot).

leading edge: the front edge of the wing as viewed from below.

litter: fallen plant material, such as twigs, leaves and needles, that forms a distinct layer above the soil, especially in forests.

lore: the small patch between the eye and the bill.

molting: the periodic replacement of worn out feathers (often twice a year).

morphology: the science of form and shape.

nape: the back of the neck.

neotropical migrant: a bird that nest in the Seattle area, but overwinters in the New World tropics.

niche: an ecological role filled by a species.

open country: a landscape that is primarily not forested.

parasitism: a relationship between two species where one benefits at the expense of the other.

phylogenetics: a method of classifying animals that puts the oldest ancestral groups before those that have arisen more recently.

pishing: making a sound to attract birds by saying *pishhh* as loudly and as wetly as comfortably possible.

polyandrous: having a mating strategy where one female breeds with several males.

polygynous: having a mating strategy where one male breeds with several females.

raptor: a carnivorous (meat-eating) bird; includes eagles, hawks, falcons and owls.

rufous: rusty red in color.

speculum: a brightly colored patch in the wings of many dabbling ducks.

squeaking: making a sound to attract birds by loudly kissing the back of the hand, or by using a specially design squeaky bird call.

talons: the claws of birds of prey.

understorey: the shrub or thicket layer beneath a canopy of trees.

References

American Ornithologists' Union. 1983. *Check-list of North American Birds*. 6th ed. American Ornithologists' Union, Washington, D.C.

American Ornithologists' Union. 1993. Thirty-ninth supplement to the American Ornithologists' Union *Check-list of North American Birds*. Auk 110:675–82.

American Ornithologists' Union. 1995. Fortieth supplement to the American Ornithologists' Union *Check-list of North American Birds*. Auk 112:819–30.

Ehrlich, P.R., D.S. Dobkin and D. Wheye. 1988. *The Birder's Handbook*. Fireside, New York.

Evans, H.E. 1993. *Pioneer Naturalists: The Discovery and Naming of North American Plants and Animals*. Henry Holt and Company, New York.

Farrand, J., ed. 1983. *The Audubon Society Master Guide to Birding*. Vols. 1–3. Alfred A. Knopf, New York.

Gotch, A.F. 1981. *Birds: Their Latin Names Explained*. Blandford Press, Dorset, England.

McCaskie, G., P. De Benedictis, R. Erickson and J. Morlan. 1988. *Birds of Northern California: An Annotated Field List*. 2nd ed., rev. Golden Gate Audubon Society, Berkeley.

Mearns, B., and R. Mearns. 1992. *Audubon to Xantus: The Lives of Those Commemorated in North American Bird Names*. Academic Press, San Diego.

National Audubon Society. 1971–1995. *American Birds* Vols. 25–48.

Peterson, R.T. 1990. *A Field Guide to the Western Birds*. 3rd ed. Houghton Mifflin, Boston.

Reader's Digest Association. *Book of North American Birds*. The Reader's Digest Association, Pleasantville, New York.

Richmond, J. 1985. *Birding Northern California*. Mount Diablo Audubon Society, Walnut Creek, California.

Robbins, C.S., B. Brunn and H.S. Zim. 1966. *Birds of North America*. Golden Press, New York.

Santa Clara Valley Audubon Society. 1990. *Birding at the Bottom of the Bay*. 2nd ed. Santa Clara Valley Audubon Society, Palo Alto.

Scott, S.S. 1987. *Field Guide to the Birds of North America*. National Geographic Society, Washington, D.C.

Sequoia Audubon Society. 1996. *San Francisco Peninsula Birdwatching*. Rev. ed. Sequoia Audubon Society, San Mateo, California.

Stokes, D., and L. Stokes. 1996. *Stokes Field Guide to Birds: Western Region*. Little, Brown and Co., Boston.

Terres, J.K. 1995. *The Audubon Society Encyclopedia of North American Birds*. Wings Books, New York.

Checklist of San Mateo County Birds

This checklist includes a total of 306 species recorded at least 10 times in San Mateo County and its offshore waters. The full checklist (including 'accidental' species) originally appeared in *San Francisco Peninsula Bird-watching* (Sequoia Audubon Society 1996), and it was compiled for the Sequoia Audubon Society by Peter J. Metropulos in January, 1996.

Symbols used in this list are defined as follows:

Seasons
W = Winter (mid-December through February)
Sp = Spring (March through early June)
Su = Summer (mid-June through July)
F = Fall (August through December)

Breeding Status
@ = Regular breeder (nests each year)
Δ = Irregular breeder (few nesting records for the county; nests infrequently)
(?) = Suspected breeder (nesting confirmation lacking)
+ = Former breeder (no nesting records in recent years)

Abundance
C = Common to abundant in appropriate habitat (always present, in large numbers)
F = Fairly common (always present, in moderate to small numbers)
U = Uncommon (usually present, in small numbers)
R = Rare (observed in very small numbers, and perhaps not in each year)
X = Extremely rare (fewer than 10 records of occurence in season indicated)
L = Local (restricted to a small portion of the county, or to a few locations, during season indicated)
e = erratic (may occur in substantially larger or smaller numbers than indicated during certain years)

Introduced species (nesting species originally released from captivity) are listed in italics. This checklist does not include 'accidental' species (recorded fewer than 10 times ever in San Mateo County and its offshore waters). A blank line separates each family of birds on the list.

Bird Name	W	Sp	Su	F
☐ Red-throated Loon	F	F	R	F
☐ Pacific Loon	F	C	U	F
☐ Common Loon	F	F	R	F
☐ Pied-billed Grebe @	F	F	U	F
☐ Horned Grebe	F	F	X	F
☐ Red-necked Grebe	R	R		R
☐ Eared Grebe	F	F	X	F
☐ Western Grebe	C	C	U	C
☐ Clark's Grebe	F	F	R	F
☐ Black-footed Albatross		U	U	R
☐ Laysan Albatross		R		
☐ Northern Fulmar	Fe	Ue	X	Ue
☐ Pink-footed Shearwater	X	F	F	F
☐ Buller's Shearwater	X		R	F
☐ Sooty Shearwater	R	C	C	C
☐ Short-tailed Shearwater	R	R		R
☐ Black-vented Shearwater	Re	Re	X	Re
☐ Fork-tailed Storm-Petrel		R		R
☐ Leach's Storm-Petrel		R	R	R
☐ Ashy Storm-Petrel		X	U	U
☐ Black Storm-Petrel			R	U
☐ American White Pelican	U	R	R	U
☐ Brown Pelican	U	U	C	C
☐ Double-crested Cormorant @	C	F	FL	C
☐ Brandt's Cormorant @	C	C	FL	C
☐ Pelagic Cormorant @	F	F	F	F
☐ American Bittern @	R	R	RL	R
☐ Great Blue Heron @	F	U	U	F
☐ Great Egret @	F	U	UL	F
☐ Snowy Egret @	F	F	FL	F
☐ Cattle Egret @	R	R		R
☐ Green Heron @	R	R	RL	R
☐ Black-crowned Night-Heron @	F	F	FL	F
☐ Tundra Swan	R	X		X
☐ Greater White-fronted Goose	R	X		X

Bird Name	W	Sp	Su	F
☐ Snow Goose	R	R	X	X
☐ Ross' Goose	X	X	X	X
☐ Brant	R	C	R	U
☐ Canada Goose @	F	F	UL	F
☐ Wood Duck @	U	U	RL	U
☐ Green-winged Teal	F	F		F
☐ Mallard @	C	F	F	C
☐ Northern Pintail @	C	U	RL	C
☐ Blue-winged Teal	R	R	X	R
☐ Cinnamon Teal @	U	F	UL	F
☐ Northern Shoveler Δ	F	U	RL	F
☐ Gadwall @	F	U	UL	F
☐ Eurasian Wigeon	R	X		R
☐ American Wigeon	C	U	X	F
☐ Canvasback	C	F	R	C
☐ Redhead	R	R	X	R
☐ Ring-necked Duck	F	U	X	F
☐ Greater Scaup	C	C	R	C
☐ Lesser Scaup Δ	C	C	R	C
☐ Black Scoter	U	U	R	U
☐ Surf Scoter	C	C	U	C
☐ White-winged Scoter	F	F	R	F
☐ Harlequin Duck	RL	RL	RL	RL
☐ Oldsquaw	R	R	X	R
☐ Common Goldeneye	F	F	X	F
☐ Barrow's Goldeneye	UL	RL		RL
☐ Bufflehead	C	F	X	F
☐ Hooded Merganser	UL	RL		RL
☐ Common Merganser Δ	R	R	XL	R
☐ Red-breasted Merganser	F	F	R	F
☐ Ruddy Duck @	C	F	UL	F
☐ Turkey Vulture @	F	F	F	F
☐ Osprey	R	R	X	R
☐ White-tailed Kite @	U	R	RL	U
☐ Bald Eagle +	RL	RL	XL	RL
☐ Northern Harrier @	U	U	UL	U
☐ Sharp-shinned Hawk @	U	U	RL	U
☐ Cooper's Hawk @	U	U	U	U
☐ Red-shouldered Hawk @	U	U	U	U
☐ Broad-winged Hawk	X	X		R
☐ Red-tailed Hawk @	F	F	F	F
☐ Ferruginous Hawk	R	X		R
☐ Rough-legged Hawk	Re	Re		Re
☐ Golden Eagle +	R	R	R	R

Bird Name	W	Sp	Su	F
❑ American Kestrel @	F	F	F	F
❑ Merlin	U	R		R
❑ Peregrine Falcon △	R	R	R	R
❑ Prairie Falcon	X	X		X
❑ *Ring-necked Pheasant* @	RL	RL	RL	RL
❑ *Wild Turkey* △	RL	RL	RL	RL
❑ California Quail @	C	C	C	C
❑ Black Rail	X			X
❑ Clapper Rail @	UL	UL	UL	UL
❑ Virginia Rail @	F	F	U	F
❑ Sora △	U	U	XL	U
❑ Common Moorhen △	R	RL	RL	R
❑ American Coot @	C	C	U	C
❑ Black-bellied Plover	C	C	U	C
❑ Pacific Golden-Plover	R	R	X	R
❑ American Golden-Plover				R
❑ Snowy Plover @	UL	RL	RL	UL
❑ Semipalmated Plover	F	F	R	F
❑ Killdeer @	C	F	F	C
❑ American Black Oystercatcher @	UL	UL	UL	UL
❑ Black-necked Stilt @	F	F	UL	F
❑ American Avocet @	C	C	UL	C
❑ Greater Yellowlegs	F	F	R	F
❑ Lesser Yellowlegs	R	R	X	U
❑ Solitary Sandpiper		X		X
❑ Willet	C	C	U	C
❑ Wandering Tattler	U	U	R	U
❑ Spotted Sandpiper △	U	U	RL	U
❑ Whimbrel	F	F	R	F
❑ Long-billed Curlew	F	F	R	F
❑ Marbled Godwit	C	C	U	C
❑ Ruddy Turnstone	U	U	R	U
❑ Black Turnstone	C	C	U	C
❑ Surfbird	F	F	R	F
❑ Red Knot	FL	FL	XL	FL
❑ Sanderling	C	C	U	C
❑ Semipalmated Sandpiper		X	X	R
❑ Western Sandpiper	C	C	U	C
❑ Least Sandpiper	C	C	U	C

Bird Name	W	Sp	Su	F
❑ Baird's Sandpiper		X	X	R
❑ Pectoral Sandpiper		X	X	R
❑ Rock Sandpiper	RL	RL		RL
❑ Dunlin	C	C	X	C
❑ Short-billed Dowitcher	C	C	R	C
❑ Long-billed Dowitcher	C	C	R	C
❑ Common Snipe	U	U		U
❑ Wilson's Phalarope		X	R	U
❑ Red-necked Phalarope		C	R	C
❑ Red Phalarope	Ue	Ue	X	Ue
❑ South Polar Skua		X	X	X
❑ Pomarine Jaeger	R	U	R	U
❑ Parasitic Jaeger	X	U	R	U
❑ Long-tailed Jaeger			X	R
❑ Franklin's Gull	X	X	X	X
❑ Bonaparte's Gull	F	C	R	F
❑ Heermann's Gull △	R	R	C	C
❑ Mew Gull	C	F		C
❑ Ring-billed Gull	C	C	U	C
❑ California Gull	C	C	F	C
❑ Herring Gull	F	F	X	F
❑ Thayer's Gull	U	U		U
❑ Western Gull @	C	C	C	C
❑ Glaucous-winged Gull	C	C	U	C
❑ Glaucous Gull	R	R		X
❑ Black-legged Kittiwake	Ue	Ue	Re	Ue
❑ Sabine's Gull		Ue	Re	Re
❑ Caspian Tern @	X	F	F	F
❑ Elegant Tern	X	R	Ue	Fe
❑ Common Tern		R	X	U
❑ Arctic Tern		Ue	X	Ue
❑ Forster's Tern @	F	C	F	C
❑ Least Tern +		RL	RL	RL
❑ Black Tern	X	X	X	X
❑ Common Murre +	C	C	C	C
❑ Pigeon Guillemot @	R	F	F	F
❑ Marbled Murrelet @	U	F	UL	F
❑ Xantus' Murrelet		X	X	R
❑ Ancient Murrelet	Ue	Ue	X	Ue
❑ Cassin's Auklet △	F	F	U	F
❑ Rhinoceros Auklet △	F	F	U	F
❑ Tufted Puffin (?)		R	R	R
❑ Horned Puffin	X	R		

Bird Name	W	Sp	Su	F
Rock Dove @	C	C	C	C
Band-tailed Pigeon @	F	F	F	F
Mourning Dove @	C	C	C	C
Barn Owl @	U	U	U	U
Western Screech-Owl @	F	F	F	F
Great Horned Owl @	F	F	F	F
Northern Pygmy-Owl @	F	F	F	F
Burrowing Owl @	R	RL	RL	R
Long-eared Owl Δ	X	XL	XL	X
Short-eared Owl Δ	Re	Re	RL	Re
Northern Saw-whet Owl @	U	U	UL	U
Common Poorwill Δ	X	UL	UL	R
Black Swift @		R	RL	R
Vaux's Swift @	X	F	UL	U
White-throated Swift @	U	U	U	U
Anna's Hummingbird @	C	C	C	C
Rufous Hummingbird		F	U	F
Allen's Hummingbird @	F	C	C	U
Belted Kingfisher @	U	U	U	U
Lewis' Woodpecker	Re	Re		Re
Acorn Woodpecker @	F	F	F	F
Red-naped Sapsucker	R	X	X	R
Red-breasted Sapsucker Δ	U	U	XL	U
Nuttall's Woodpecker @	F	F	F	F
Downy Woodpecker @	F	F	F	F
Hairy Woodpecker @	F	F	F	F
Northern Flicker @	C	F	F	C
Pileated Woodpecker @	RL	RL	RL	RL
Olive-sided Flycatcher @		C	C	U
Western Wood-Pewee @		C	C	F
Willow Flycatcher		X		R
Hammond's Flycatcher	X	X		X
Pacific-slope Flycatcher @	X	C	C	C
Black Phoebe @	F	F	F	F
Say's Phoebe	F	U		F
Ash-throated Flycatcher @		F	F	U
Tropical Kingbird	X	X		R
Western Kingbird (?)		R	XL	R

Bird Name	W	Sp	Su	F
Horned Lark @	U	UL	UL	U
Purple Martin Δ		R	RL	R
Tree Swallow @	U	F	F	F
Violet-green Swallow @	U	C	C	C
Northern Rough-winged Swallow @	X	F	F	F
Bank Swallow @	X	FL	FL	U
Cliff Swallow @		C	C	F
Barn Swallow @	X	C	C	C
Steller's Jay @	C	C	C	C
Scrub Jay @	C	C	C	C
Yellow-billed Magpie +	X	X	X	X
American Crow @	F	F	FL	F
Common Raven @	F	F	F	F
Chestnut-backed Chickadee @	C	C	C	C
Plain Titmouse @	C	C	C	C
Bushtit @	C	C	C	C
Red-breasted Nuthatch @	Fe	Fe	U	Fe
White-breasted Nuthatch @	F	F	F	F
Pygmy Nuthatch @	C	C	C	C
Brown Creeper @	C	C	C	C
Rock Wren Δ	R	RL	RL	R
Bewick's Wren @	C	C	C	C
House Wren @	R	U	UL	U
Winter Wren @	F	F	F	F
Marsh Wren @	F	F	FL	F
American Dipper @	RL	RL	RL	RL
Golden-crowned Kinglet @	Fe	Fe	FL	Fe
Ruby-crowned Kinglet	C	C		C
Blue-gray Gnatcatcher @	R	U	UL	R
Western Bluebird @	U	U	U	U
Swainson's Thrush @		C	C	C
Hermit Thrush @	C	C	FL	C
American Robin @	C	C	C	C
Varied Thrush Δ	Ce	Ce	XL	Ce

Bird Name	W	Sp	Su	F
❑ Wrentit @	C	C	C	C
❑ Northern Mockingbird @	C	C	C	C
❑ California Thrasher @	C	C	C	C
❑ American Pipit	C	C		C
❑ Cedar Waxwing	C	C	X	C
❑ Phainopepla		X	X	X
❑ Loggerhead Shrike @	U	U	RL	U
❑ *European Starling* @	C	C	C	C
❑ Solitary Vireo @	X	F	F	F
❑ Hutton's Vireo @	C	C	C	C
❑ Warbling Vireo @	X	C	C	C
❑ Tennessee Warbler	X	X	X	R
❑ Orange-crowned Warbler @	U	C	C	C
❑ Nashville Warbler	R	R		R
❑ Northern Parula Δ		X	R	X
❑ Yellow Warbler @	X	F	F	C
❑ Chestnut-sided Warbler		X	X	R
❑ Magnolia Warbler		X	X	R
❑ Yellow-rumped Warbler @	C	C	UL	C
❑ Black-throated Gray Warbler @	R	F	F	F
❑ Townsend's Warbler	C	C		C
❑ Hermit Warbler	R	F	FL	F
❑ Prairie Warbler	X	X		R
❑ Palm Warbler	R	X		R
❑ Blackpoll Warbler		X		R
❑ Black-and-white Warbler	R	X	X	R
❑ American Redstart	X	X	X	R
❑ Northern Waterthrush	X		X	R
❑ MacGillivray's Warbler @	X	U	UL	U
❑ Common Yellowthroat @	F	F	FL	F
❑ Hooded Warbler		X	X	X
❑ Wilson's Warbler @	X	C	C	C
❑ Yellow-breasted Chat		R	X	X
❑ Western Tanager @	X	F	UL	F
❑ Rose-breasted Grosbeak Δ	X	X	R	X
❑ Black-headed Grosbeak @	X	C	C	C
❑ Lazuli Bunting @		F	F	U
❑ Indigo Bunting Δ	X	X	X	X
❑ Spotted Towhee @	C	C	C	C
❑ California Towhee @	C	C	C	C
❑ Rufous-crowned Sparrow @	RL	RL	RL	RL
❑ Chipping Sparrow @	X	F	F	U
❑ Clay-colored Sparrow	X	X		R
❑ Lark Sparrow @	R	UL	UL	U
❑ Savannah Sparrow @	C	F	F	C
❑ Grasshopper Sparrow @	X	F	F	R
❑ Fox Sparrow	C	C		C
❑ Song Sparrow @	C	C	C	C
❑ Lincoln's Sparrow	F	F		F
❑ Swamp Sparrow	R	X		R
❑ White-throated Sparrow	R	R		R
❑ Golden-crowned Sparrow	C	C		
❑ White-crowned Sparrow @	C	C	C	C
❑ Dark-eyed Junco @	C	C	C	C
❑ Lapland Longspur	X	X		R
❑ Bobolink		X	X	R
❑ Red-winged Blackbird @	C	F	F	C
❑ Tricolored Blackbird @	F	F	UL	F
❑ Western Meadowlark @	C	F	F	C
❑ Yellow-headed Blackbird	X	X	X	X
❑ Brewer's Blackbird @	C	C	C	C
❑ Brown-headed Cowbird @	U	C	C	F
❑ Hooded Oriole @	X	F	F	U
❑ Bullock's Oriole @	R	F	F	U
❑ Purple Finch @	C	C	C	C
❑ House Finch @	C	C	C	C
❑ Red Crossbill Δ	Ue	Ue	Re	Ue
❑ Pine Siskin @	C	F	F	C
❑ Lesser Goldfinch @	C	C	C	C
❑ Lawrence's Goldfinch Δ	X	Re	Re	X
❑ American Goldfinch @	C	C	C	C
❑ Evening Grosbeak	Re	Re	X	Re
❑ *House Sparrow* @	C	C	C	C

Index of Common Names

Boldface page numbers refer to primary, illustrated entries.

Index of Scientific Names

This index only references primary species treatments.

About the Authors

When he's not out watching birds, frogs or snakes, Chris Fisher researches endangered species management and wildlife interpretation in the Department of Renewable Resources at the University of Alberta. The appeal of western wildlife and wilderness has led to many travels, including frequent visits with the birds of the Pacific coast. By sharing his enthusiasm and passion for wild things through lectures, photographs and articles, Chris strives to foster a greater appreciation for the value of our wilderness.

Joseph Morlan is an instructor of ornithology in the Community Services division of City College of San Francisco, where he has been teaching birding classes at all levels for 20 years. He is also co-author of *Birds of Northern California* and a regular contributor to various ornithological journals. He is a member of the California Bird Records Committee and is on the editorial board of *Western Birds*. Joe's primary interest is in bird distribution and field identification. He is probably best known as the voice of the 'Northern California Rare Bird Alert' and its successor the 'Northern California Bird Box' (1-415-681-7422), a telephone service that keeps birders abreast of the latest bird sightings in the area.